CHRISTCHURCH PARK & IPSWICH ARBORETUM

SOUVENIR & GUIDE

Written by
DAVID MILLER

**With photography by Liz Cutting
and artwork by Erika Bűlow-Osborne and Duane Pugh**

Foreword by Anthony Cobbold

Independent Publishing Network

First published in October 2018 by Independent Publishing Network
in association with

The Friends of Christchurch Park, Ipswich
www.focp.org.uk

A catalogue record of this book is available from the British Library

Miller, David
Christchurch Park & Ipswich Arboretum: Souvenir & Guide

Printed by Tuddenham Press Ltd.

ISBN 978-1-78926-112-7

All proceeds from the sale of this book will go to the Friends of Christchurch Park
for the benefit of Ipswich Arboretum and Christchurch Park.

By the same author
Ipswich Arboretum: A History and Celebration
Published in 2014 by Gresham Publications
in association with
The Friends of Christchurch Park

For more details of other books published by the Friends of Christchurch Park go to
www.focp.org.uk

FRONT COVER Christchurch Mansion and London Plane (*Platanus × hispanica*)
and the early 13th century Seal of Christchurch, Ipswich drawn by J. S. Corder 1893

TITLE PAGE View looking north-west over Snow Hill, Christchurch Park

BACK COVER The Wilderness Pond, Christchurch Park

For Rebecca and Nicholas

INTRODUCING

the outstanding artwork of

DUANE PUGH

with fifteen studies of CHRISTCHURCH

especially commissioned by the author for this book

Duane was born in Ipswich in 1986 and still lives and works in the town. He started drawing at the age of four and later studied Art and Design at Suffolk College and Fine Art at the University of Suffolk. He loves to draw any subject but his greatest passion is portraits. Duane is available for commission work and can be contacted on duanepugh19861986@gmail.com.

viii

THE GREAT WAR
1914   1919
1939 WORLD   WAR II 1945

RESTORED AND RE-ERECTED
IN 2016 IN MEMORY OF
DR JOHN BLATCHLY MBE
D. P '18

**A message from Alan Prickett
Managing Director
Ransomes Jacobsen Ltd.**

I am very pleased to support David's latest book *Christchurch Park & Ipswich Arboretum: Souvenir & Guide.*

Ransomes Jacobsen's long history began in 1789 when Robert Ransome (1753-1830), founder of the Ipswich-based agricultural machinery company that became the world-famous Ransomes, Sims and Jefferies, set up an iron-foundry business with just £200 opposite St. Mary-at-the-Quay Church in Ipswich, before moving soon after to a disused maltings in St. Margaret's Ditches (now Old Foundry Road), just a minute or two's walk from Christchurch Park, which was then owned by William Fonnereau (1732-1817), son of Claudius Fonnereau.

Ransomes has a number of interesting and historic links with Christchurch Park and Ipswich Arboretum. As David tells us in this book, Ipswich owes the creation of its first public park (the Arboretum) to James Allen Ransome (1806-75) who in 1847 first proposed the idea and location of a plot of arable land and meadow adjoining the western boundary of the then private Christchurch Park as a "*suitable place, in which a healthful and harmonious recreation could be carried out... beneficial to all classes of the town*". James Allen was a grandson of Robert and he became a Partner in the firm in 1829 and Senior Partner in 1864.

David has also advised me that James Edward Ransome (1839-1905), another grandson of Robert and a cousin of James Allen, and John Robert Jefferies (c.1840-1900), (he married James Allen's youngest daughter Mary), who became joint Chairmen of Ransomes, Sims and Jefferies in 1886, were both subscribers to the first ever guide book about Christchurch, *Christchurch or Withepole House – A Brief Memorial*, written and illustrated by J. S. Corder and published in 1893 when the future of the Park and Mansion looked to be most uncertain. It is therefore very fitting that we support this latest guide 125 years later.

On a more personal level, David recalls his late-father Tony's choice of lawnmower in the Arboretum was the Ransomes Mk 2 Matador. The legendary Mk 1 was, of course, famously in 1959 driven non-stop from Edinburgh Castle to Hyde Park, London (375 miles) down the A68 and A1 in four days and three nights by a team of five students from Hatfield Technical College to demonstrate its incredible reliability.

Over the last few years Ransomes have taken a great interest in David's work in the Arboretum and Park, and have been delighted to support it. During that time, we have sponsored a number of specimen trees, built and donated a number of specially made iron tree guards and commemorative plaques and we printed David's three tree guides in 2015, 2016 and 2017. I congratulate him on his latest book and hope that its success will further assist the excellent work of the Friends of Christchurch Park.

Alan Prickett
September 2018

PERFECT EVERY BLADE.

The Ransomes Mastiff.

The Ransomes Mastiff is the premier sports surface and pitch heavy duty roller mower powered by a reliable 9hp petrol engine. Able to produce a distinctive 91cm pristine striped finish, the Ransomes Mastiff continues its legacy of a better, more consistent cut – day in and day out.

Arrange a demonstration by contacting your local dealer at:
www.ransomesjacobsen.com or call 01473 270000

RANSOMES®

Contents

ACKNOWLEDGEMENTS

The author would like to thank the following:

Erika Bŭlow-Osborne for her Scherenschnitte
Anthony Cobbold for the Foreword
Liz Cutting for her photographs
Sarah Miller for proof-reading
Duane Pugh for his artwork
Reg Snook for permission to use the portrait on page 92

Colchester and Ipswich Museum Service for permission to use the portrait on page 3

Ransomes Jacobsen Ltd. for generously supporting this book

FOREWORD

I am delighted to have been invited to introduce David Miller's excellent new book about Christchurch; a better qualified author would be hard to find, not least because of his strong family connection. Indeed, it is exactly that intangible but very real power of "those who have gone before us" that lies behind the invitation I have just accepted. You will read how the Mansion was saved for the people of Ipswich by the generosity of my relative, Felix Cobbold and how in his will he left a further £20,000 for the purchase of artworks.

Just nine years ago, to mark the centenary of Felix's death, we held a party in the Great Hall during which over one hundred family and friends faced his portrait and toasted his memory. The portrait by the Honourable John Collier was paid for by grateful public subscription but to mark the centenary there was a trail around the rooms of the Mansion which identified over one hundred works of art which had been purchased, either in whole or in part, from the Felix Thornley Cobbold bequest. Also, when you visit, you will see three fine carved overmantels from the Half Moon Inn, the Tankard Inn and the Neptune Inn, all famous Ipswich pubs in their time, donated by Felix's family to grace his gallery. The latter, known as the Thomas Eldred overmantel marks his circumnavigation of the world as Lord Cavendish's navigator in 1588. Other gifts include a clock and a portrait of the legendary Margaret Catchpole by her author Richard Cobbold which has always intrigued me as he was only 4 years old when she was transported to Australia!

The Ipswich Society's first choice for the location of their blue plaque in honour of Felix was of course the Mansion itself but fixtures to Grade 1 listed buildings are not allowed and two alternatives were suggested; an inscription on a flagstone outside the front door of the Mansion or the Reg Driver Centre. Somehow being trampled on by thousands of visitors in all weathers lacked appeal which left only the modern Reg Driver Centre. Initially I was against this site on the grounds that it wasn't even there in Felix's day. On rethinking it, however, I realised that Felix was always forward thinking, always championed the underdog and always wanted the best for men and their families. He would have thoroughly approved of the Reg Driver Centre which now proudly bears his blue plaque, prominently, for all to see.

There are many examples of Felix's philanthropy but there is one which best illustrates his philosophy. He left some 700 acres in the Felix Thornley Cobbold Agricultural Trust which was divided into allotments to further his belief that every man should own the means to feed his family. This worked well for a while but agriculture was moving in the direction of combination and consolidation which forced the trustees to negotiate new terms with the Charity Commission. The focus of the trust was switched to the education of young farmers through the example of a demonstration farm, Stanaway, and nearby Otley College stands on land which was part of the original bequest.

Felix was elected Mayor of Ipswich in Queen Victoria's jubilee year, 1896 and he organised a number of celebrations for old and young, all of which took place here in Christchurch Park.

1

Two family members before him and another two after him held the office of Mayor of Ipswich and their plaques are there for all to see on the Mayors' Walk.

The Lodge on Cobbold Point at Felixstowe was Felix's home where he cultivated a magnificent garden; as a connoisseur of natural beauty he would have been well pleased by the Christchurch Park of today noting the care lavished upon it and appreciating particularly the unfettered devotion of David Miller to the Arboretum. I suggest David is driven, as I am in developing The Cobbold Family History Trust, by a fundamental gratitude and admiration for "those who have gone before us". The Mansion, the Park, the Arboretum and David's new book amply illustrate the power of such motivation.

Anthony Cobbold
Keeper, The Cobbold Family History Trust
September 2018

Felix Cobbold JP, MP (1841-1909) by the Hon. John Collier, 1897, OBE, RP, ROI (1850-1934)
(Courtesy of Colchester and Ipswich Museums, IPSMG: R.1960-181)
As Felix's memorable year in office as Mayor drew to a close this portrait of him was
unveiled in the Great Hall at Christchurch Mansion. Commissioned by the Council, it was
paid for by public subscription with 890 subscribers. The portrait still has pride of place in
the Great Hall and shows Felix relaxing in the lounge of The Lodge at Felixstowe.

3

Welcome from the Chairman

Welcome to Christchurch Park and Ipswich Arboretum.

It is 29 years since Ipswich Borough Council published their excellent *Christchurch Mansion & Park Ipswich – An Illustrated Souvenir* so I thought it was about time I wrote an up-to-date memento. IBC's guide from 1989 focussed primarily on the beautiful Grade I-listed Tudor Mansion, as does of course the more recent and equally delightful booklet *Christchurch Mansion Ipswich* published in 2015 by our friends at the Friends of the Ipswich Museums.

It is also 125 years since the architect and artist John Shewell Corder (1856-1922), fearing for the future of the Mansion, wrote and illustrated *Christchurch or Withepole House – A Brief Memorial*, which was published by S. H. Cowell, Buttermarket, Ipswich in 1893; a magnificent hardback volume and the most treasured of the Christchurch guides in my collection.

I hope that the guide I have written will serve a slightly different purpose by looking across the whole 83-acre Park and Arboretum and showcasing a number of interesting features and subjects for the visitor, which of course includes Christchurch Mansion, but also many other attractions some of which were not present in 1989 and even 2015. If you require a detailed study of Edmund Withepole's (or even Withypoll's or Withipoll's) jewel in our town's historic past I thoroughly recommend FoIM's above title and of course Corder's if you can source one!

I am indebted to Anthony Cobbold, Liz Cutting, Erika Bülow-Osborne, Duane Pugh and Alan Prickett, Managing Director of Ransomes Jacobsen Ltd. I cannot thank Liz enough for her stunning photographs which bring this guide to life. Liz and I have collaborated on a number of projects including my first book *Ipswich Arboretum – A History and Celebration* (2014), my three tree guides (2015, 16 & 17), tree information boards and leaflet *Ipswich Arboretum* (2017). Alan and Ransomes Jacobsen Ltd. have supported our work for a number of years and their latest assistance means that Christchurch will benefit even more from the sale of this book.

Our Park and Arboretum is managed by IBC and we are fortunate to have an extraordinarily dedicated team based at the Reg Driver Visitor Centre led by Park Manager Nigel Campbell, who care for and look after this very special place. In addition to Nigel and his team of gardeners, there are many other people who work here whose passion and commitment is invaluable including the RDVC Receptionists, Arboriculturalists, Wildlife and Education Rangers and Park Patrol to name a few. Christchurch benefits from an equally dedicated small army of volunteers plus may I say a very active and supportive FoCP – more about us later.

If you are a local resident or regular visitor you will no doubt be familiar with much, if not all of the content in this guide. If you are visiting Christchurch Park or Ipswich Arboretum for the first time today, I hope you enjoy your visit and find the following pages of interest and use.

With very best wishes,

David Miller
Chairman, Friends of Christchurch Park
September 2018

1. A Brief History of Christchurch

Christchurch Park can today be found in the centre of Ipswich but it actually lies just outside the North Gate of the town's medieval boundary. In William the Conqueror's Domesday Book (1086), in the Half Hundred of Ipswich on land controlled by Roger Bigot for the King, the survey records an Anglo-Saxon church, Holy Trinity, to the west of Thingstede Way (now Bolton Lane) in possession of 26 acres of land: "*In the said Borough, Alnulfus the priest has a church, Holy Trinity, to which belongs twenty-six acres in alms*". This was to become the site of Holy Trinity Priory (also known as Christ Church), a Priory of Regular (or Black) Canons of St. Augustine, founded a little prior to 1177 and largely endowed by Norman Gastrode fil Eadnothi. It accommodated a Prior and six or seven Canons but the original building was destroyed by fire soon after its erection and entirely rebuilt in 1194 by John de Oxenford, Bishop of Norwich. The Priory was endowed with manors, lands and rents in many parishes in and around Ipswich, all named and confirmed by a grant of King John dated 11 January 1204.

The early 13th century Seal of Christchurch, Ipswich probably adopted after the Charter of King John (drawn by J. S. Corder 1893)
"Sigillum Ecclesie Christi Gippewicensis"
(Seal of Christ Church, Ipswich)

By 1291 the value of the possessions of the Priory was £47 17s. 4½d and at the end of 13th century, as the population around it grew, the Canons began to build an adjacent church dedicated to St. Margaret. The Priory became a rich and powerful establishment and by the time of the suppression was said to be in a very flourishing condition. When it fell victim to Henry VIII's dissolution in 1536, the Priory's value had risen to £88 6s 9d per year with an estate of 643 acres (260 hectares). Most of the buildings were then destroyed and the site was leased to Sir Humphrey Wingfield and Sir Thomas Rushe but the King later revoked this and transferred the property to Sir Thomas Pope. Then in 1545 it was purchased by a prominent London Merchant, Paul Withypoll who bought the estate including St. Margaret's church and some other land for £2,000. It was Paul's son Edmund who would shortly start building the house now known as Christchurch Mansion.

5

2. Christchurch Mansion

Location: South front is viewable from the Soane Street entrance.

Undoubtedly Ipswich's jewel in the crown, this spectacular Grade I-listed Tudor Mansion is today free for all to visit and enjoy. It has been a museum for well over 100 years and is one of only a few mansions in England which is open to the public all year long, with no entrance charge, providing you with an opportunity to discover its history, learn about the families who lived there and explore its many rooms, all of which are furnished with art and period furniture. There are also free tours offered by the Friends of the Ipswich Museums and a cafe on site.

Built by Edmund Withypoll in 1548-50 on the ruins of the Augustinian Priory of Holy Trinity, Christchurch Mansion was first known as Christchurch Withypoll and later Withypoll House, and remained in the possession of the Withypoll family for nearly one hundred years, until 1645, when it was inherited by Elizabeth, the daughter and heir of Sir William Withypoll, and wife of Leicester Devereux who inherited the title 6th Viscount Hereford in 1649. Leicester was responsible for many alterations to the house and gardens and it also remained a home for the Devereux family for nearly one hundred years until it was sold in 1735 by Price Devereux, 10th Viscount Hereford, for £11,500 to Claude Fonnereau, a successful London Merchant, and son of a Huguenot refugee, descended from the Earls of Yvery in Normandy. The Fonnereaus stayed at Christchurch for over 150 years during which time a number of additions and alterations were made to the principal rooms. The last member of the Fonnereau family to live here was William Neale Fonnereau who in 1892 put the estate on the market for £50,000.

6

For nearly 350 years Christchurch Mansion was home to just three families and during that time had entertained Elizabeth I (in 1561 and 1579), Charles II (1662) and Prince Albert (1851). However, its future became most uncertain when it was placed on the market. In April 1892 Ipswich Corporation consulted the people of Ipswich with a local referendum of registered owners and ratepayers as to whether the town should purchase the Christchurch estate (by then reduced by Fonnereau to £42,000). 2,169 papers were returned blank, 87 spoiled, 5,110 votes were against and 3,784 in favour. Two years later Fonnereau sold Christchurch for £36,000 to a property syndicate and part of the estate along Bolton Lane and Park Road was immediately resold and built upon. This prompted the Council to purchase 51 acres of the Park but the purchase did not include the Mansion or the grounds to the south and west and the syndicate drew up plans for the demolition of the Mansion to build more houses.

Christchurch Mansion was saved by Felix Thornley Cobbold (1841-1909), arguably the town's greatest philanthropist, who then bought the Mansion and wrote to the Mayor on 23 October 1894 "*Having contracted to purchase Christchurch House..., I desire to offer the property to the inhabitants of Ipswich as a free gift, subject to certain conditions.*" The conditions were that "*the main structure of the house be preserved in its integrity*", and that the Council purchase the remainder of the Park for the town. The offer was accepted and the gift completed on 23 February 1895. On 24 April 1895 Christchurch Park was officially opened to the public and on 18 April 1896 Christchurch Mansion was opened as a local Archaeological Museum and Picture Gallery. In his will, from an estate of £407,790 15s 9d, Cobbold left a £20,000 trust fund to the Mayor and Burgesses of the Borough of Ipswich, the interest of which were to be used to preserve the building and purchase pictures and other works of art.

3. The Wolsey Art Gallery

Location: At the back of Christchurch Mansion

The Wolsey Pageant was organised by the Corporation and staged on the lawns in front of Christchurch Mansion from 23 to 28 June 1930 to honour the memory of the greatest of all Ipswichians, Thomas Wolsey (c.1475-1530) on the 400th anniversary of his death. Celebrations were based on Shakespeare's *Henry VIII* and consisted of eight performances, one every evening from Monday to Saturday with two additional performances on the Wednesday and Saturday afternoons. The Patron was His Royal Highness the Prince of Wales, who flew in to Ipswich Airport from Northolt in his personal Westland Wapiti Ia, J9095 (with an RAF fighter escort) on 26 June to attend the Thursday performance. The Prince stayed about fifteen minutes, having to squeeze a dozen engagements into his five-hour visit which included opening the Aerodrome, touring the town centre and visiting Ransomes, Sims and Jefferies.

The Pageant was on a grand scale. In the souvenir programme the Mayor Arthur Clouting (the town's first Labour Mayor) wrote *"That the people of Wolsey's native town and county have wished to be associated with this memorial is proved by their magnificent response. Thousands – and the word is used in its strict meaning – have, according to their opportunities, co-operated in the common cause of ensuring that the Pageant shall be worthy"*. Over 1,500 names were listed in the programme with Mayor Clouting commenting that *"The names of a few are recorded..., but many valuable helpers must necessarily be omitted"*.

The following year a purpose-built art gallery (partially funded by the Pageant) was built at the back (North side) of Christchurch Mansion. It was named the Wolsey Art Gallery as a memorial to the Cardinal and opened on 19 October 1932. Hailed as the most prestigious and important temporary exhibition space in Ipswich, it has, since then, received major refurbishment twice (1989 and 2011) and is used to house, amongst others, the collection of works by John Constable and Thomas Gainsborough. The Constable collection is the most significant collection of works by the artist outside London. The Fonnereaus are also believed to have been among the earliest of Gainsborough's patrons.

From 7 February 2015 to 31 January 2016 the Gallery exhibited one of the greatest masterpieces of British art, Constable's *Salisbury Cathedral from the Meadows*, 1831. This work was bought by Tate in May 2013 for £23.1 million as part of Aspire, a partnership between Tate and four other galleries (National Museum Wales, National Galleries of Scotland, Colchester and Ipswich Museums Service and Salisbury and South Wiltshire Museum) with assistance from the Heritage Lottery Fund, the Art Fund (with a contribution from the Wolfson Foundation), The Manton Foundation, and Tate Members, enabling the work to go on view across the UK.

From 13 October 2017 to 11 March 2018 Ipswich was treated to another superb exhibition *Thomas Wolsey: Ipswich's Greatest Son*. The highlight was the four magnificent bronze Wolsey Angels commissioned by Wolsey in 1524 for his tomb from the Italian sculptor Benedetto da Rovezzano and created between 1524 and 1529. Purchased by the Victoria and Albert Museum three years ago for £5 million, with assistance from the Heritage Memorial Fund, the Art Fund and the Friends of the V&A, the splendid Angels exhibition at the Wolsey Art Gallery was the first time they had been displayed together outside their London home, thanks to the V&A's generosity and support from the Friends of the Ipswich Museums.

Coming soon: Auguste Rodin's *The Kiss* will be on display here from 24 November 2018 to 28 April 2019 on loan from the Tate Collection, as the centre-piece of the *Kiss and Tell: Rodin and Suffolk Sculpture* exhibition.

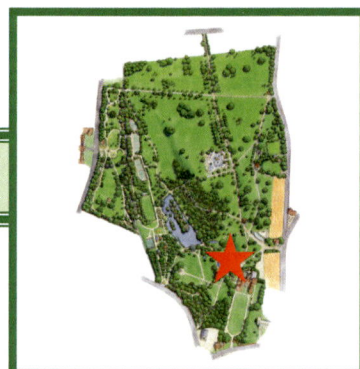

4. The Round Pond

Location: Next to Christchurch Mansion

The Park's natural springs which once supplied water to the medieval town also fed a number of ponds in the Park, including today's Round Pond, which is older than the Tudor Mansion and dates from monastic times. The Round Pond is believed to have originally been one of the Priory fish ponds, used to feed the Canons with carp, tench, roach and gudgeon. After the Mansion was built, the Pond was used by the owners as a Mirror Pond to reflect their home. On Kirby's 1735 plan of Christchurch (see inside back cover) the Pond is labelled the 'Bason'.

During the Spring of 2007 the Pond was emptied, dredged and cleaned as part of the Heritage Lottery Fund (HLF) Restoration of the Park (see Timeline on page 86 for further details of the Restoration). During the clean-up it was discovered that between eight and ten feet of silt had built up since the last time it was fully dredged in the 1920s, and partially cleaned in the 1980s. Tons of silt was removed and hundreds of historical artefacts were found including coins, bullets from both World Wars, musket balls, regimental badges, rings, pocket watches, whistles and children's toys. Many of these items are on display in the Reg Driver Visitor Centre. A dry season followed completion of the work which significantly affected the Pond's natural filling ability and so in January 2008 an iconic 1953 Green Goddess owned by Suffolk Fire Engine Services was employed to speed up the refilling process by pumping some 200,000 gallons from the Wilderness Pond, which naturally fills much quicker. In late 2018 a new fountain is scheduled to be added to the Pond. This will have some practical uses to reduce the build-up of unwanted surface material and help move any floating litter to the edge where it can be more easily collected. It will also have a timer enabling it to be turned off at night for feeding bats. The project will be led by IBC with a number of funding partners including FoCP.

5. The Wilderness Pond

Location: A short walk west from the Reg Driver Visitor Centre

One of the most popular areas of the Park, the Wilderness Pond is believed to have been created in around 1567 by Edmund Withypoll, although the natural springs which still feed this pond once fed a number of other ponds close to the once formal gardens to the west of the Mansion. The overflow from the Park's ponds ran down Dairy Lane (now Fonnereau Road) and into what is now Northgate and Upper and Lower Brook Streets. In fact, Withypoll's periodic draining of his ponds was once the subject of complaint by the Corporation. However by the time the Fonnereaus were living here, the owners were prepared to let out the ponds in times of emergency to assist in firefighting in the town. On Kirby's map the Wilderness Pond was known as 'Dovehouse Pond' and it also clearly shows the western edge of the Pond as being straight but this was altered and extended to its current form during the landscaping for the Arboretum. In February 2007, as part of the HLF Restoration, the Wilderness Pond was drained and dredged, in advance of the Round Pond. The Pond is up to ten feet deep, but in some areas seven feet of silt had accumulated, leaving very little depth of water. Today the Pond is well known for its Mandarin ducks, Mallards, Moorhens, Canada geese, Cormorants and of course Terence (see page 30). You might even spot a Kingfisher at the north end or glimpse a Muntjac on one of the islands. Occasionally, something really exciting can turn up, like a Goosander!

6. Champion Trees

Location: Various locations, see map to the right

Christchurch Park contains a good number of veteran trees some of which are amongst the largest and most majestic in Suffolk. Included in this section are four 'Champion Trees' of Christchurch, so-called because they are the biggest and oldest of their species in the Park. Please note that tree measurements in this guide were recorded in 2014 and 2015.

London Plane *Platanus × hispanica* (see front cover photo). The Park's largest plane towers over the Soane St. entrance with a height of **31 metres (102 feet)**. This spectacular tree has a trunk circumference (at 1.5 m) of **594 cm (19 feet)** and is probably over 200 years old.

English Oak *Quercus robur* (see photo below left). This magnificent specimen located south-west of the Ancient Avenue/Mayors' Avenue cross-roads stands **23.1 metres (76 feet)** tall, has a trunk circumference (at 1.5 m) of **670 cm (22 feet)** and is probably around 500 years old.

English Yew *Taxus baccata* (see photo below right). This is the oldest tree in the Park and can be found south-east of the Cenotaph. Standing **14.2 metres (47 feet)** tall it has a trunk circumference (at 1.2 m) of **447 cm (15 feet)** and is believed to be over 600 years old.

Sweet Chestnut *Castanea sativa* (see photo opposite). This giant is probably over 500 years old and has the greatest girth of any tree in the Park. Located north-west of the Ice House, it has a vast trunk circumference (at 1.5 m) of **820 cm (27 feet)** and is **18.3 metres (60 feet)** tall.

12

7. The Ice House

Location: A short walk north from the Reg Driver Visitor Centre

Unless you know where to look you could easily walk right by this Grade II listed building without even noticing it! Ice houses are buildings (often underground, as is the case here) used to store ice throughout the year. In 18th century England, long before the invention of the refrigerator, ice was regarded as a luxury and ice houses became something of a status symbol on the wealthiest estates. These structures were often sited close to natural sources of winter ice, in this case, the Round and Wilderness Ponds, and during the colder months, ice would be cut from the ponds and packed into the ice house and stacked between layers of insulation (straw or sawdust) to make one huge solid freezing mass. If ice was in short supply, compacted snow could be used instead. The straw, bricks and earth would ensure the contents of the ice house remained frozen, often until the following winter ensuring a reliable way to cool wine, keep meat fresh and prepare cold desserts in the Mansion throughout the year.

The Christchurch Ice House was built c.1735 when Claude Fonnereau acquired the estate and made many improvements to the Park and Mansion. There is a brick vaulted antechamber to the entrance on the north side and the brick-lined straight-sided underground chamber is around 30 feet deep, with a crowned brick dome overhead. The earth covering the ice houses was often planted with trees and ivy to help keep the area cool and dry and entry was restricted to prevent cold air from escaping. By the 19th century ice was being shipped over from Norway and with the development of the railway, transportation of ice became the norm and ice houses obsolete.

8. Ipswich Martyrs' Memorial

Location: Next to the Reg Driver Visitor Centre

The Martyrs' Memorial remembers nine Protestant martyrs from Ipswich and nearby villages, who were burned to death for their beliefs in the mid-sixteenth century. In 1902, the book *Seventeen Suffolk Martyrs* by Nina Frances Layard was published by Smiths, Suitall Press. This brought the martyrs' history to local public attention and in November of that year the Mayor of Ipswich William John Catchpole called a Public Meeting to discuss the possibility of erecting a memorial. A committee was formed which included Layard and subscriptions were raised. The monument was designed by the architect H.T. Edwards of the Art Memorial Company, West Norwood, London and was unveiled on Wednesday 16 December 1903 by the Very Rev. Henry Wace, D.D., the Dean of Canterbury. It stands 27 feet (8.2 m) high and 10 feet 6 inches (3.2 m) square at the base. The committee originally intended for the memorial to be placed on the Cornhill where six of the nine martyrs were executed. However, this was not possible so it was situated where it stands today. The names of the martyrs are: N. Peke of Earl Stonham (burned 1538), Kerby of Ipswich (1546), Robert Samuel of East Bergholt (1555), Agnes Potten of Ipswich (1556), Joan Trunchfield of Ipswich (1556), John Tudson of Ipswich (1556), Alexander Gouch of Woodbridge (1558), Alice Driver of Grundisburgh (1558) and William Pikes of Ipswich (1558). Listed Grade II. As well as the names and dates of execution the following inscriptions are present:

THE NOBLE ARMY OF MARTYRS PRAISE THEE

THIS MONUMENT IS ERECTED TO THE MEMORY OF NINE IPSWICH MARTYRS WHO FOR THEIR CONSTANCY TO THE PROTESTANT FAITH SUFFERED DEATH BY BURNING

OH MAY THY SOLDIERS FAITHFUL, TRUE AND BOLD FIGHT AS THE SAINTS WHO NOBLY FOUGHT OF OLD AND WIN WITH THEM THE VICTORS CROWN OF GOLD ALLELUIA

9. Ipswich War Memorial (Cenotaph)

Location: A short walk south from the Wilderness Pond

The *Programme of the Proceedings* for the unveiling of the 'Christchurch Park Memorial' show that it was to be unveiled by the Right Hon. The Earl of Derby, K.G., P.C., G.C.B., G.C.V.O., (Secretary of State for War during World War I) on Saturday 3 May 1924. Unfortunately, Derby was taken ill and Rear Admiral Sir Richard Webb and Lieutenant General Sir Aylmer Hunter-Watson deputised at short notice. The Memorial consists of a Cenotaph backed by a Screen Wall and was designed by Edward Adams, A.R.I.B.A., a Manchester architect, whose winning design was chosen by the War Memorial Committee from over 200 submissions from all over the country. Work to construct the Memorial was awarded to Messrs. Collins and Curtis, a local company of Handford Road, whose partners were ex-service men. The Portland stone was said to be of particularly fine quality. The bronze-work and name panels were by Manchester sculptors Messrs. Earp, Hobbs and Miller.

The town's annual Service of Remembrance is held in front of the Grade II listed Memorial every November. Today, the Cenotaph bears the following inscriptions: *OUR GLORIOUS DEAD 1914-1919* and *1939-1945*. At the foot of the Cenotaph is a bronze roll of military equipment and the *Programme of the Proceedings* described it thus:

THE LARGE CAST BRONZE TROPHY OF ARMS, SYMBOLIZES THE ACCOUTREMENTS OF THE WAR LAID ASIDE. IT IS BUILT UP OF EQUIPMENT, INCLUDING REGIMENTAL STANDARDS, BUNDLES OF LANCES, MACHINE GUNS AND STOKES TRENCH GUN [invented by Sir Wilfred Scott-Stokes (1860-1927), Managing Director of the Ipswich engineering firm Ransomes and Rapier] *WITH TRIPOD AND SHELLS. THE WHOLE IS BOUND TOGETHER WITH CORDS AND DRAPED WITH THE UNION JACK AND ST. GEORGE'S BANNER. IN THE CENTRE IS DEPICTED THE PERSONAL EQUIPMENT OF THE SOLDIER – HAVERSACK, TRENCHING TOOL, WATER BOTTLE AND GAS MASK, INTERWOVEN WITH STEMS OF OAK AND LAUREL LEAVES AND SURMOUNTED BY A RIFLE AND HELMET.*

Below the roll of military equipment is a further inscription: *THE GREAT WAR 1914 1919* and *WORLD WAR II 1939 1945*. On the reverse of the Cenotaph is a bronze attachment with the inscription: *IN GRATEFUL MEMORY OF THE MEN OF IPSWICH WHO GAVE THEIR LIVES FOR THEIR COUNTRY THIS MEMORIAL AND THE HOSPITAL WAR MEMORIAL WING WERE ERECTED BY THEIR FELLOW CITIZENS.*

The unveiling ceremony was attended by many thousands and included the hymns *God of our fathers, known of old* (Kipling) and *O God, our help in ages past* (Watts, Croft). A performance of *The Reveille* (Elgar) by the Ipswich Male Voice Choir followed the *Last Post* which was played by the Buglers of the 2nd Batt. Suffolk Regiment. After the Unveiling, Scripture Reading, Dedication, Period of Silence, Prayers and Wreath-laying, the ceremony concluded with the *Bugle Reveille* (2nd Batt. Suffolk Regiment), The Blessing by The Lord Bishop of the Diocese, the National Anthem and the Procession.

It is estimated that about 10,000 Ipswich men joined the Colours for the First World War and the Screen Wall behind the Cenotaph, containing the bronze name panels, shows that at least 1,481 made the great sacrifice. In all, the East Suffolk and Ipswich Hospital (Anglesea Road) received 7,777 casualties up to May, 1919.

On 16 May 2004 five new plaques were unveiled on the Screen Wall with the names of 626 Ipswichians who died during World War II. The extension was constructed by Paul Templeton of Suffolk Masonry Services, who had also worked for 20 years for Collins and Curtis. On 10 May 2009, the Screen Wall was further updated with an additional plaque *Conflicts Post-1945* listing six service personnel who lost their lives in conflicts since the Second World War:

LT. SWINBANKS, B.	*Royal Engineers*	*Korea*	*1951*
PTE. MCDONALD, R.H.	*Royal Norfolk Rgt.*	*Korea*	*1952*
L/Bdr. BRETTELL, M.A.	*Royal Artillery*	*Korea*	*1952*
FO. BANYARD, K.W.	*Royal Air Force*	*Cyprus*	*1956*
PTE. BARNES, G.I.	*Parachute Rgt.*	*N. Ireland*	*1979*
PTE. MCCLURE, A.J.	*Royal Anglian Regt.*	*Afghanistan*	*2007*

Did you know? The most common dates for the First World War on war memorials are 1914-1918 which commemorates the year that the war started and the year the armistice was declared, on 11 November 1918. However, the Christchurch Park War Memorial uses the dates 1914-1919. This is not unusual. The 1919 date refers to the year in which the Treaty of Versailles was signed. Although the armistice ended the fighting, there followed a further six months of negotiations at the Paris Peace Conference before the peace treaty was signed on 28 June 1919 in Versailles which officially ended the state of war between Germany and the Allied Powers.

10. Boer War Memorial

Location: South-east of the Ipswich War Memorial

The Suffolk Soldiers Memorial for the South African Conflict 1899-1902 (The Boer War) was unveiled on the Cornhill by General Sir John French at 3.15 pm on Saturday 29 September 1906. Designed and made by Albert Toft (1869-1949), this memorial stands 15 feet 6 inches high. The bronze statue is life-sized (6 feet) and depicts a soldier in uniform with head bowed and rifle reversed, as at the graveside of a comrade. It was moved to its current position close to the Ipswich War Memorial in 1924 to allow more space on the Cornhill for trams that needed to turn. This feat required 50 men to pull it on rollers up the hill to the Park. There are similar memorials by Toft in Cambridge and Bury St Edmunds, but this is the only one in which the soldier has his head bowed. The stepped square plinth has a bronze plaque attached to each of the four faces of the upper stage. These plaques detail rank, name and Regiment of 284 soldiers who lost their lives. Excellent research by Jean Austin and Martin Edwards revealed some surprising statistics; over 175 of these soldiers either died of disease, enteric (typhoid) fever or dysentery. There were also some unexpected causes of death including Private Robert Taylor of the Suffolk Regiment who was killed by lightning on 10 November 1901 near Senekal and Private J. Plumb also of the Suffolk Regiment who died when he was hit by a train at Myfontein on 7 May 1902. Listed Grade II, the front plaque also bears the following dedication:

*SUFFOLK SOLDIERS
MEMORIAL
ERECTED BY
SUFFOLK PEOPLE
AS A MONUMENT
TO SUFFOLK SOLDIERS WHO
LOST THEIR
LIVES IN THE SOUTH
AFRICAN WAR 1899-1902*

11. Birds and other Wildlife

Not surprisingly, the Park and Arboretum is a haven for birds and other wildlife, including a number of well-known non-native species such as Canada goose, Mandarin, Grey squirrel (displacing the original red population), Muntjac and Brown rat. In Reg Snook's excellent *Portrait of the Birds* (published by Gresham and FoCP in 2014), we learn that over the previous fifty years a total of 115 species of bird have been recorded in, or flying over, Christchurch Park. This total is divided into two lists; *Birds you have a good chance of seeing here* (53 species) and *Other birds that have been seen here* (62 species). This list excludes ornamental pinioned waterfowl. Reg also reminds us that two pairs of Wrynecks bred in the Park in 1948, as reported in *The Birds of Suffolk* by William H. Payne (1962). Possibly one of the oldest records of birds in this Park, and not included in the 'official' list is that of a pair of Black-necked swans which came from a zoo in the Black Forest and were presented to the Park in 1898 by the Mayor of Ipswich Robert Stocker Paul. Early postcards also reveal that other exotic birds kept here at this time included a Sarus crane, the world's tallest flying bird, with a standing height of up to 1.8 metres (c.6 feet), White stork, Peafowl and Egyptian geese. To bring the above list up to date Reg has advised that since publication of his book a further nine species take the total to 124; Goosander, Raven, Short-eared owl, Rough-legged buzzard, Honey buzzard, Golden oriole, Alpine swift, Coot, and the most recent addition, Ring-necked parakeet, which was recorded in this Park for the first time at 08.00 on 28 November 2017.

In Richard Stewart's equally informative *The Butterflies in Christchurch Park* illustrated by Liz Cutting (published by FoCP in 2016), we read that 24 species of butterfly have been recorded here: Brimstone, Brown argus, Comma, Common blue, Essex skipper, Gatekeeper, Grayling, Green-veined white, Holly blue, Large skipper, Large white, Meadow brown, Orange-tip, Painted lady, Peacock, Purple hairstreak, Red admiral, Ringlet, Small copper, Small skipper, Small tortoiseshell, Small white, Speckled white and Wall brown. Other notable insects recorded include Stag beetle (*Cervus lucanus*) and Bee wolf (*Philanthus triangulatum*).

The UK is home to eighteen species of bat, and Sue Hooton, Chairperson of the Suffolk Bat Group has reported that in the last five years of joint SBG/FoCP Bat Walks (2013-17) she has recorded seven species in the Park: Common pipistrelle, Soprano pipistrelle, Nathusius' pipistrelle, Noctule, Serotine and Daubenton's plus one unidentified *Myotis* species, possibly Natterer's. Some bats are simple to identify with a bat detector (heterodyne) as they echolocate at different frequencies (heard as irregular rapid clicks on the detector). The frequencies at which you are most likely to receive the strongest signals for our Park species are: Common pipistrelle (45 kHz), Soprano pipistrelle (55 kHz), Nathusius' pipistrelle (39 kHz), Noctule (20-25 kHz), Serotine (27 kHz), Daubenton's (45 kHz) and Natterer's (50 kHz). When some are harder to differentiate, then size, wing shape, flight patterns and habitat may also be considered.

Finally, Pat Gondris has recently been observing bees in the Butterfly Garden and has recorded Honey bee (*Apis mellifera*) and the following Bumble-bees: Red-tailed (*Bombus lapidarius*), Tree (*B. hypnorum*), Garden (*B. hortorum*), White-tailed (*B. lucorum*), Buff-tailed (*B. terrestris*), Common Carder (*B. pascuorum*), and possibly Early (*B. pratorum*). FoCP would be very interested to hear from anyone who believes they can add to any of these lists, or who has compiled lists of other wildlife in this Park.

Robin (*Erithacus rubecula*)

Wren (*Troglodytes troglodytes*)

Juvenile Long-tailed tit (*Aegithalos caudatus*) and below, a female Mallard (*Anas platyrhynchos*)

Goosander (*Mergus merganser*) and below, a Cormorant (*Phalacrocorax carbo*)

23

Male Mandarin (*Aix galericulata*) and below, a female Mandarin

Mandarin duckling (*Aix galericulata*) and below, Canada goslings (*Branta canadensis*)

Blackbird (*Turdus merula*) and below, a Mistle thrush (*Turdus viscivorus*)

Dunnock (*Prunella modularis*) and below, a Starling (*Sturnus vulgaris*)

Chaffinch (*Fringilla coelebs*) and below, a Grey squirrel (*Sciurus carolinensis*)

28

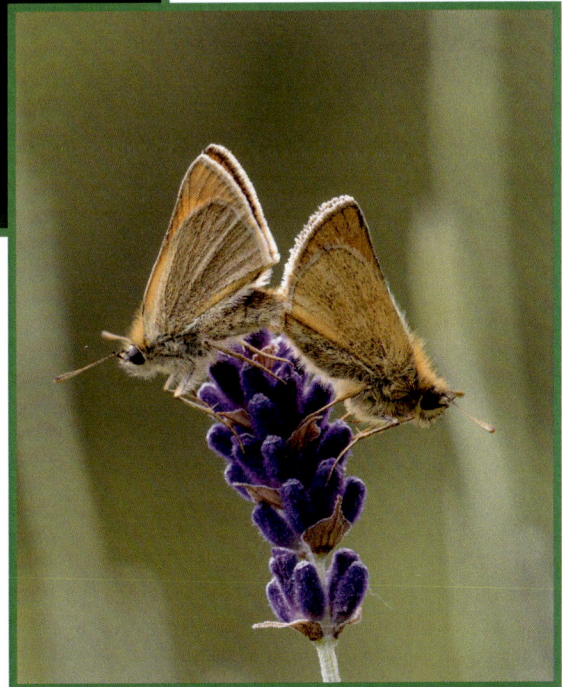

Clockwise from top left: Orange-tip butterfly (*Anthocharis cardamines*), Peacock (*Aglais io*), Small skippers paired (*Thymelicus sylvestris*) and Small copper (*Lycaena phlaeas*).

12. Mabel and Terence

Location: English oak tree near Westerfield Road entrance (Mabel) and Wilderness Pond (Terence)

The Park's most famous resident in recent years has undoubtedly been the Tawny owl (*Strix aluco*) first sighted by dog walkers in the Park on 21 September 2008 in a hole near the top of an old English Oak tree close to the Westerfield Road entrance. Named 'Mabel' after schoolchildren were invited to make suggestions, she quickly achieved celebrity status and over the following nine years has been photographed in the same hole during the daytime by countless birders and other members of the public and has even appeared in national newspapers and wildlife magazines. During those nine years she has helped the Parks Department by feeding on the Park's population of Brown rats together with House and Wood mice and probably an assortment of small to medium-sized birds, young Grey squirrels, bats, moles, frogs, insects, worms and possibly ducklings and young rabbits.

Each year Mabel would disappear in the breeding season and we now know that she was in fact still present in the same tree, just deeper in the hole raising chicks. It is likely that she did in fact successfully breed on a number of occasions and some very lucky Park visitors have even spotted her mate and offspring. She proved to be remarkably tolerant of some of the Park's noisier activities such as the Ipswich Transport Museum's Ipswich to Felixstowe Historic Vehicle Road Run in May and the 11th Ipswich Scout Group's fireworks display in November. Sadly, we don't think Mabel has been seen since September 2017. Tawny owls can live for up to twenty years in captivity but that age is almost certainly likely to be less in the wild.

Probably the second most famous resident in the Park is a non-native species, a Red-eared slider (*Trachemys scripta elegans*), a species of terrapin native to the USA and South America, which has been, since long before the arrival of Mabel, regularly observed on sunny days basking on a protruding log in the Wilderness Pond. Named 'Terence' by former Park Manager Sam Pollard it has like Mabel, become something of a celebrity (appearing in local newspapers) and is now arguably the town's best-known and best-loved pet! Sam Pollard believes that Terence was probably bought as a pet during the Teenage Mutant Hero Turtles craze and then became too big for its owners and so was released by them into the Wilderness Pond. Given that the peak in the franchise's popularity was in the late 1980s and early 1990s, Terence may well be 25 years old or older, but is certainly over 20 years old. Certain individuals of this species have been known to live for over 40 years and reach more than 40 cm (16 inches) in length.

When the Wilderness Pond was scheduled to be drained for cleaning in 2007 as part of the HLF Restoration Project, Terence's welfare became a subject of great concern to the Park's regular visitors. However, their concerns were allayed when Park gardener Trevor Sergeant leapt into action and rescued Terence who then enjoyed a ten-week holiday at a local terrapin rescue centre before being returned to the pond after it had been cleaned out. Although Terence will be feeding on certain native species such as fish, frogs (and tadpoles), snails, crickets, aquatic plants, also probably dead birds and possibly even young ducklings, the impact of his presence on the Park's eco-system is considered to be minimal. Recently there have been reports that Terence has a friend or even a mate, and this has now been confirmed by Liz Cutting's photograph opposite. However, although we are not actually sure of their gender, it is considered most unlikely that a pair could successfully breed in the Wilderness Pond as they would require sustained periods of hot weather in order for any eggs to hatch.

31

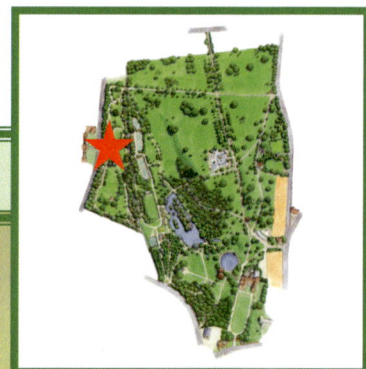

13. Ipswich Arboretum

Location: Main entrance is on Henley Road opposite Ipswich School

Ipswich owes the creation of its Arboretum to Councillor James Allen Ransome (1806-75) who on 9 November 1847 in the Town Hall Council Chamber first proposed both the idea and location of a plot of two fields known as 'Upper Bolton' to the west of the Rev. William Charles Fonnereau's then privately owned Christchurch Park as a "*suitable place, in which a healthful and harmonious recreation could be carried out... beneficial to all classes of the town*".

James Allen (known as J. Allen or just Allen) was the grandson of Robert Ransome (1753-1830), founder of the Ipswich-based agricultural machinery company that became the world-famous Ransomes, Sims and Jefferies. J. Allen became a Partner in the family firm in 1829 and Senior Partner in 1864 but his energies were not just confined to the family firm. He became one of the most prominent men in Ipswich and for thirty years served the corporate body. In 1844 he was elected a Liberal representative of the St. Margaret's Ward and was re-elected seven times. In 1865 he was made an Alderman, a position he held until his death.

Ipswich Arboretum was designed by Yorkshire nurseryman William Pontey (c.1792-1862) and landscaped in March 1851, but was however, first opened the same year to fee-paying subscribers only. Two years later the eight acre 'Upper' portion was opened for the general public but the five acre 'Lower' Arboretum remained a private subscription garden for the town's wealthier classes for over 70 years until 1922 when it was purchased by the Corporation for £1,568 14s 3d. The Upper Arboretum was also purchased by the Corporation in 1928 for £8,500 when the Fonnereaus' original 75-year lease expired.

The Victorian Prospectus of 'The Ipswich Arboretum Society' gave the following introduction: *The formation of a place for healthful out-door recreation, accessible to all classes of the inhabitants of this rapidly increasing town, has long been needed. In the year 1848 a public meeting was convened, at which time the unanimous desire prevailed that an eligible spot might be selected, not only adapted for carrying out to the fullest extent this highly important object, but which, whilst administering to the health and rational enjoyment of the people of Ipswich, should be rendered, by its appropriation to the science of Arboriculture, not less worthy the support and patronage of the county at large.* It went on to state that the object of the Society "*shall be the collection and scientific classification of all such species of trees and shrubs as will endure this climate*". This object remains the primary purpose of Ipswich Arboretum today.

The Arboretum enjoys a reputation for horticultural and arboricultural excellence. In the 1980s it played a pivotal role in the town's successes in Britain in Bloom – a nationwide horticultural competition organised by the RHS, and first run by the British Tourist Authority in 1964 following a pilot the previous year. As the centrepiece of the town's campaign the Arboretum helped Ipswich win the Regional Final on four consecutive years (1983-86), the English Final in 1986 and a prestigious award in 1985 for the best carpet-bedding display in Britain.

Did you know? Ipswich Arboretum is the oldest public park in Ipswich. Many Ipswichians consider Christchurch Park to be the town's first 'Public Park', but when the Public (Upper) Arboretum opened its gates for all to use in 1853, Christchurch was still privately owned by the Fonnereau family and did not officially open to the public for another 42 years.

Above: Atlas Cedar *Cedrus atlantica* in the Upper Arboretum with a height of **21 metres (69 feet)** and a trunk circumference (at 0.6 m) of **493 cm (16 feet)**.
Below: The two tallest trees in the Upper Arboretum are (left) a Giant Redwood *Sequoiadendron giganteum* (planted in 1863) with a height of **28.1 metres (92 feet)** and Deodar Cedar *Cedrus deodara* (planted in 1864) with a height of **27 metres (89 feet)**.

33

Top row from left: Chinese Witch Hazel *Hamamelis mollis*, Cork Oak *Quercus suber*, Japanese Larch *Larix kaempferi*, Lawson Cypress *Chamaecyparis lawsoniana*.
Middle row from left: Serbian Spruce *Picea omorika*, Maidenhair Tree *Ginkgo biloba*, Cider Gum *Eucalyptus gunnii*, Wollemi Pine *Wollemia nobilis*.
Bottom row from left: Western Red Cedar *Thuja plicata*, Handkerchief Tree *Davidia involucrata*, Tulip Tree *Liriodendron tulipifera*, Monkey Puzzle *Araucaria araucana*.

Low's Fir *Abies concolor* var. *lowiana*, planted in 1984 and has already reached **17.1 metres (56 feet)** with a trunk circumference (at 1.2 m) of **240 cm (8 feet)**.

Coast Redwood *Sequoia sempervirens*, the tallest tree in the Lower Arboretum at **26.3 metres (86 feet)** with a trunk circumference (at 1.5 m) of **290 cm (9.5 feet)**.

14. Sampson's Clock

Location: Arboretum Lodge, Henley Road entrance

At the main entrance to the Arboretum opposite Ipswich School stands the oldest of the remaining entrance lodges around the Park. When the Arboretum Lodge was built in 1853 it did not have its distinctive clock turret. This addition was made 26 years later in 1879 and was a gift of George Green Sampson (1804-85), a surgeon at the East Suffolk and Ipswich Hospital who was also a magistrate for 34 years and was elected Mayor of Ipswich on four occasions (1838, 1846, 1870 and 1871). The turret was erected by Messrs. John B. and Frederick Bennett, Builders, of Church Street, Ipswich according to the plans of Edward Buckham, the Borough Surveyor and the clock which had a face two feet in diameter was installed by Thomas Ward, a watchmaker and jeweller, of Queen Street.

Twenty years ago, the clock was vandalised with a catapult and stopped working. On 9 December 2016, a new clock was installed by David Bearcroft and was funded by the FoCP. The new clock has an electric movement replacing the hand wound mechanism and the new dial bears the name G. G. Sampson and the date 1879 as requested by David Miller in honour of the original patron and to add historical interest for visitors today.

15. Over 100 Years of Carpet Bedding

Location: Upper Arboretum, Henley Road entrance

In 1901 James Mann, a 32 year old from Playford, Suffolk (pictured below left) was appointed Head Gardener to the Upper Arboretum and shortly after he started a popular tradition that has continued for more than a century, and is much loved to this day. Mann's contribution to the Arboretum was immense: he inaugurated the Mayors' Walk in the Lower Arboretum and designed the Lower Arboretum Rock Gardens using sarsen stones that were discovered during the excavations for the Ipswich wet dock in the early 1840s. Mann would also later become the Corporation's Parks Superintendent but he is best remembered for his exceptional carpet bedding displays in the Upper Arboretum which have continued with equally delightful displays by Head Gardeners since, including Tom Reed and Tony Miller (see opposite).

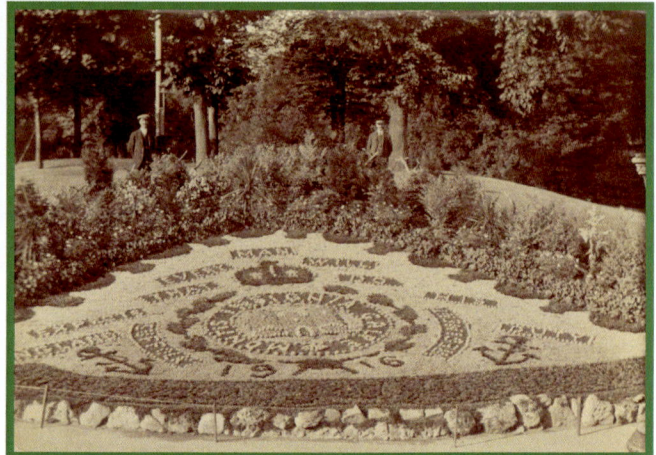

Top right, James Mann and his wife Fanny admire his Flower Clock which depicted closing time. Below are two of Mann's war-themed displays. The left image from 1915 shows Servicemen admiring a war vessel, allies flags and images of Britannia and Lord Kitchener. The right image from 1916 reads "*England Expects That Every Man Will Do His Duty*" with "*Suffolk Regiment 1916*" and the regiment's motto "*Montis Insignia Galpe*" (Badge of the Rock of Gibraltar) with an image of a castle.

In 1962 Tom Reed (Head Gardener 1955-66), pictured with his wife Violet, designed a carpet bed to celebrate Ipswich Town becoming Football League champions. Below, Tony Miller's (HG 1966-91) 1990 display. Inset, Tony Miller. Miller's 1985 display won an award for best carpet bedding in Britain.

39

16. The Prince's Oak

Location: Next to the Arts and Crafts Shelter, Upper Arboretum

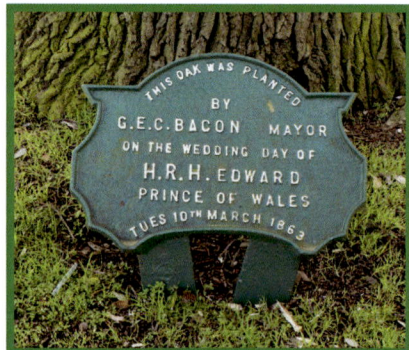

The Prince's Oak (an English Oak *Quercus robur*) was planted by the Mayor George Edgar Constantine Bacon (1813-80) on Tuesday 10 March 1863 to commemorate the marriage of His Royal Highness the Prince of Wales (later Edward VII) with the Princess Alexandra, of Denmark, at St. George's Chapel, Windsor Castle. An etching of the planting ceremony was drawn and published in May 1863 by Henry Davy (1793-1865).

Three and a half years later, on 19 September 1866, an amusing report of proceedings in a Town Council meeting can be found in the *Ipswich Journal*: Thomas Shave Gowing (1806-74), a member of the Corporation's Estate Committee entrusted with superintendence of the Arboretum, who oversaw the planting, said that he "*had been accused of planting, in the Arboretum, on the day of the Prince of Wales's marriage, an oak which was not an oak*". He begged to say that "*if any gentleman had still a doubt upon the subject he might go up to the Arboretum, and he would see the fruit of the oak upon the tree. (Laughter.)*". It is now a magnificent specimen **20.1 metres (66 feet)** tall with a trunk circumference (at 1.5 m) of **314 cm (10 feet)** and a huge crown spread of **30.5 metres (100 feet)**.

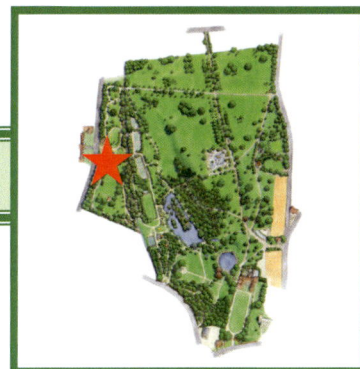

17. The Shakespearean Memorial Tree

Location: South of the Brett Drinking Fountain, Upper Arboretum

This magnificent Blue Atlas Cedar *Cedrus atlantica* 'Glauca' was planted by Cllr Thomas Shave Gowing at five o'clock on Saturday afternoon 23 April 1864 to celebrate the three hundredth anniversary of the birth of William Shakespeare (1564-1616). Unfortunately, it has sustained much damage and lost considerable height in recent storms and has even been struck by lightning but currently stands **17 metres (56 feet)** tall with a trunk circumference (at 1.5 metres) of **340 cm (11 feet)**. Between two and three thousand people attended the Arboretum on 23 April 1864 to witness the planting ceremony including several hundred children (many of whom had brought toy spades) who at the end of proceedings were asked to throw a spadeful of earth upon the roots in order that they might remember the day. After fixing the tree in place, Gowing recited the following verses which he had composed in praise of his Memorial tree:

To him, who lov'd to lie
Under the green-wood tree,
And let his fancy roam
O'er sky and earth and sea,
We dedicate this tree!

To him, whose fav'rite haunts
Were parks with ancient trees,
And sunny slopes and deer,
Rooks' nests, wild flowers, and bees,
We dedicate this tree!

To him, whose loving heart
Beat with the humblest joys,
Revelling in childhood's sports,
Its merry laugh and noise,
We dedicate this tree!

To him, who would have thought
Winding paths 'mid spreads of green,
Alive with happy groups,
A humanizing scene,
We dedicate this tree!

To him, the glorious Bard!
Who rules with mighty rhymes,
Not only English hearts
But those of other climes,
We dedicate this tree!

To him, Poetic King!
Let's willing tribute pay,
In his own coin – his thoughts,
While to his natal day,
We dedicate this tree!

A Tree Information Board written by David Miller and designed by Martin Surgey of Lifechart with photographs by Liz Cutting was erected next to this cedar on 30 August 2017. On 24 and 26 October 2017 with joint funding from FoCP and IBC, Eastwood Tree Services were contracted to carry out some 'Air-spading' and 'Terraventing' work to relieve the soil compaction around this tree's root-plate. These techniques are endorsed by Kew Gardens for root invigoration and to improve tree vitality. A top-dressing of wood chips was then applied to recreate a natural forest floor and Biochar (a carbon-rich charcoal soil improver) was added to nourish the soil, improve its structure and enhance growing conditions.

18. Rejuvenation of the Tree Collection

Location: Arboretum

Ipswich Arboretum contains over one thousand trees of several hundred different species, variants and cultivars. One third of the established trees are Holm Oak and a mix of Common Holly forms which were planted to provide year-round shelter and seclusion. Some of the other flagship mature specimens present include Atlas Cedar (including Blue), Black Cherry, Cider Gum, Coast Redwood, Common Beech, Deodar Cedar, English Oak, False Acacia, Giant Redwood, Indian Bean, Lawson Cypress, London Plane, Monkey Puzzle, Rhododendron, Tree of Heaven, Turkey Oak and Western Red Cedar. Over the last four years, David Miller and Steve Leech (IBC Tree Inspector) have planted over 200 new specimens in the Arboretum plus nearly one hundred more in the Park, worth over £60,000, nearly all of which have been funded by individual sponsors (as memorial trees), local businesses and organisations, and therefore at zero cost to IBC. Today, diversity is vital to protect against catastrophic loss from Dutch Elm Disease-type outbreaks and over the last four years, more than 130 new species and cultivars have been added to the collection; many of these cannot be seen anywhere else locally.

New plantings include eleven new oaks (Chestnut-leaved, Hungarian, Lucombe, Pondaim, Purple Sessile, Sawtooth, Scarlet, Sessile, Turner's, Variegated Turkey and Willow), nine new magnolias ('Black Tulip', 'Galaxy', 'Heaven Scent', Japanese Big-leaf, 'Leonard Messel', 'Merrill', 'Spectrum', 'Star Wars' and 'Yellow Bird'), eight new ornamental cherries ('Amanogawa', 'Amber Beauty', 'Cheal's Weeping', 'Royal Burgundy', 'Shimidsu-Sakura', 'Shirotae', 'Spire' and 'Ukon'), six new *Hamamelis* or Witch hazel ('Aphrodite', 'Arnold Promise', 'Jelena', 'Jermyn's Gold', 'Livia' and 'Vesna'), six new pines (Chinese White, Holford's, Maritime, Mexican Weeping, Montezuma and Weymouth), and five new birch (Chinese Red-barked, Monarch, Paper, Purple and Swedish). The Arboretum also has a count of ten Monkey Puzzles, eleven Giant Redwood, nine Coast Redwood and six Wollemi Pine. As a result, Ipswich Arboretum contains one of the finest new tree collections in East Anglia.

When specimen trees are planted here, they are given the very best treatment. Each is provided with a large de-compacted pit, composted manure, bone meal, controlled-release feed, mycorrhizal fungi, Biochar, irrigation pipe and a top dressing of bark mulch. Mycorrhizal fungi grow in association with the tree roots and one of their many benefits is that they greatly increase the absorptive area of the tree, effectively acting as extensions to the root system which help the tree to cope better in conditions of drought. Biochar is a carbon-rich charcoal soil improver used to nourish the soil, improve its structure and enhance growing conditions. The applications here of mycorrhizas and Biochar are a first for Ipswich Parks.

Not all of the new plantings will survive; disease, drought and unfortunately vandalism will play their part. It is also likely that we will lose many of our mature Horse Chestnut (bleeding canker) and Ash (ash dieback) in the coming decade. There are over 300 Horse Chestnut trees in the Park so their loss will be particularly noticeable. However, our proactive approach of planting a diverse range of genus will hopefully ensure that the Arboretum and Park is well-placed to provide future generations with an outstanding collection of rare and unusual trees most of which cannot be seen anywhere else in Ipswich. Visitors will find many new plantings and mature specimens now have a botanical label attached by David Miller and courtesy of the FoCP. Lists of new plantings are also available at the Reg Driver Visitor Centre.

Some of the sixty memorial trees funded by David Miller in memory of his father Tony Miller.
Top row from left: Irish Juniper *Juniperus communis* 'Hibernica', Blue Arizona Cypress *Cupressus arizonica* 'Glauca', Blue Spruce *Picea pungens* 'Super Blue', Amur Cork Tree *Phellodendron amurense*.
Middle row from left: Fastigiate Oak *Quercus robur* 'Fastigiata Koster', Incense Cedar *Calocedrus decurrens*, Southern Nettle Tree *Celtis australis*, Purple Oakleaf Beech *Fagus sylvatica* 'Rohanii'.
Bottom row from left: Turner's Oak *Quercus × turneri* 'Pseudoturneri', Turkish Hazel *Corylus colurna*, Serbian Spruce *Picea omorika*, Blue Giant Redwood *Sequoiadendron giganteum* 'Glauca'.

43

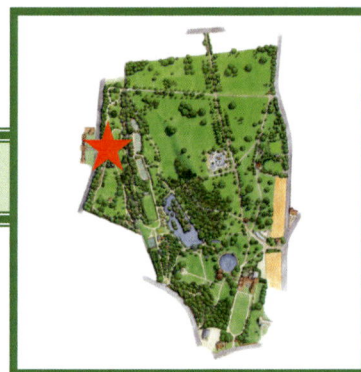

19. Brett Drinking Fountain

Location: Upper Arboretum, Henley Road entrance

On 17 October 1862 Ipswich-born John Brett (c.1801-74), a retired shoemaker, wrote to the Mayor and Corporation: *Gentlemen – Feeling a deep interest in all improvements connected with my native town, I have viewed with much satisfaction the establishment and progress of the public Arboretum, and being desirous of assisting in its improvement, I have caused to be prepared by Mr Farrow, of Carr Street, a Drinking Fountain, which I desire to have placed therein. I beg leave, therefore, to present the same for your acceptance on behalf of the town, hoping it may be the means of inducing further improvements and accommodation for the public. It is now ready for erection in any part of the grounds your Committee may think most desirable, under the direction of Mr R. M. Phipson, the Architect.*

Richard Phipson (1827-84) is best-known for the renovation of many Suffolk and Norfolk churches, with three of his most notable projects being the spires of St. Mary-le-Tower, Ipswich, St. Mary, Woolpit and St. Andrew, Great Finborough. The Fountain cost Brett £64 and on Saturday 8 November 1862, the *Ipswich Journal* reported that it was now built and was "*a very handsome little piece of architecture*": *It is a quadrangular column in the Composite style of Classic Architecture, highly and beautifully enriched with carving. It stands upon a broad double base of Portland slab; the lower portions of the structure are of Aubigny stone, and the upper and more enriched part of Causland stone. In the four facia of the column[s] are the recesses for the mouths of the fountain, which will be filled in with ornamental iron work: the water will not be kept running, but the fountain will be furnished with a tap to avoid waste. Under the recesses are the basins, formed like large columns, giving width to the structure upon the basement. The angles of the structure are adorned with pillars of Purbeck marble, the remains of that used in the improvements of Messrs. Bacon & Cobbold's bank, and kindly given by Mr [G. E. C.] Bacon for this purpose: these pillars are finished with a neat and pretty floral capital in Causland stone, the design slightly varied in each capital. The cornice and frieze-work are very effective pieces of carving. The column is surmounted with an enriched pyramid, crowned with a handsome floral finial corresponding with four pinnacles at the corners of the structure. Jewel ornaments of different coloured marble give life and effect to the whole.*

The Fountain was opened by Cllr Thomas Shave Gowing at noon on 1 May 1863 with the *Ipswich Journal* reporting that there were a large number of spectators. Gowing described the Fountain as being "*perhaps one of the handsomest in the kingdom*". Unfortunately, the Mayor George Bacon was unable to attend and his deputy Edward Grimwade (1812-86) declined the invitation remarking "*it would be a very cold subject to make a speech upon*". Gowing concluded the ceremony by reading some verses he had prepared, calling on four different classes of people to partake of the water: children, labourers, strangers and townsmen frequenting the Arboretum, and lastly ladies. At the conclusion of each stanza, representatives of each group came forward and drank, one of the four taps being devoted to each class.

This Grade II listed structure has been restored twice in recent times: in 1981 funded by the Ipswich Society, and in 2005 as the first feature to be restored (by Suffolk Masonry Services) during the HLF Restoration Project, after which it was re-opened by the Mayor, Bill Wright, 142 years after the first Mayor-free occasion. Gowing's poem was recited again, with pupils from Ipswich School and St. Margaret's Primary School taking part in the ceremony.

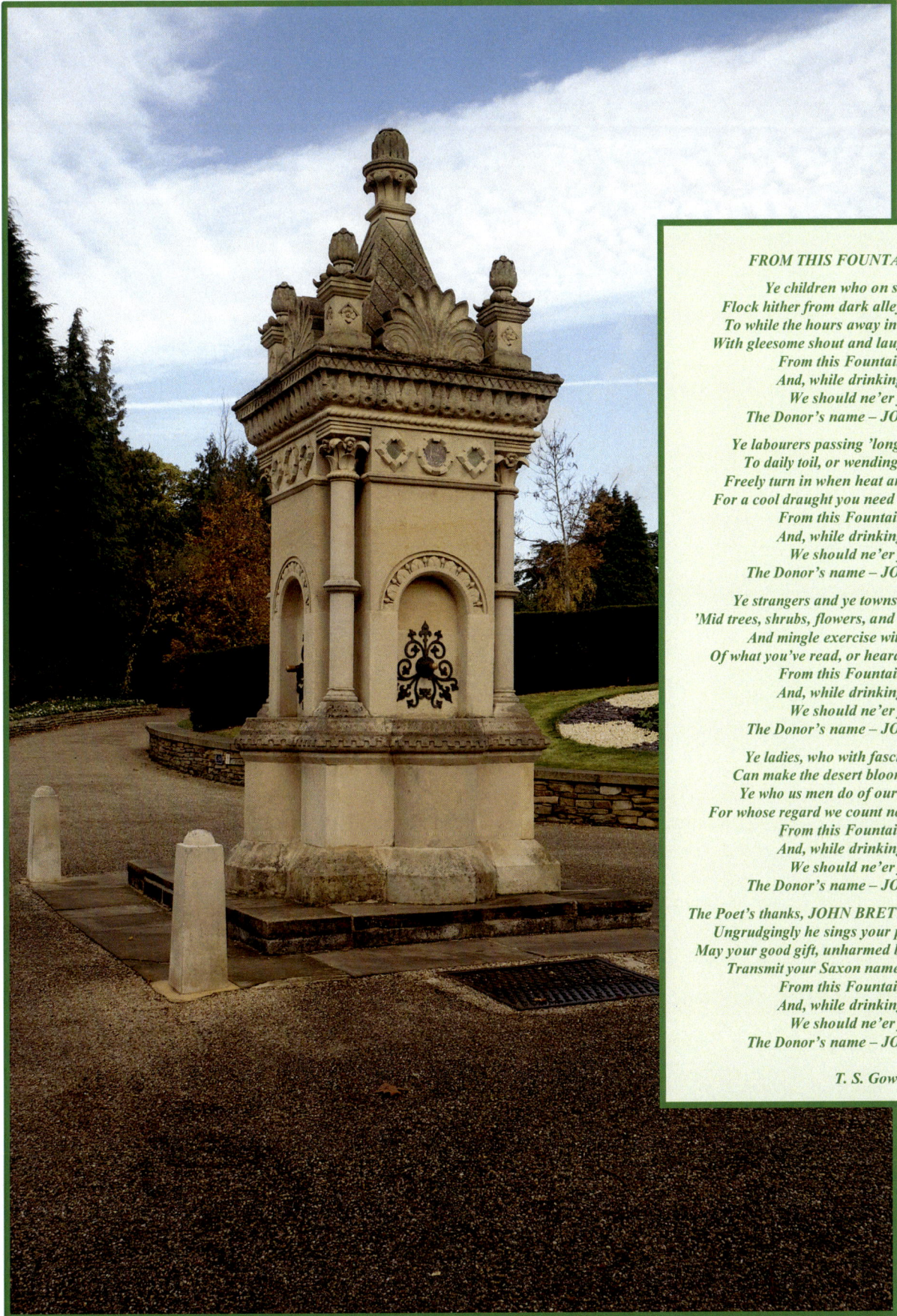

FROM THIS FOUNTAIN DRINK!

Ye children who on sunny day,
Flock hither from dark alley, court, or street
To while the hours away in sport and play,
With gleesome shout and laugh and busy feet –
From this Fountain drink,
And, while drinking, think,
We should ne'er forget
The Donor's name – JOHN BRETT.

Ye labourers passing 'long the dusty road
To daily toil, or wending weary home,
Freely turn in when heat and thirst do goad
For a cool draught you need no further roam –
From this Fountain drink,
And, while drinking, think,
We should ne'er forget
The Donor's name – JOHN BRETT.

Ye strangers and ye townsmen as ye walk
'Mid trees, shrubs, flowers, and views pleasant green,
And mingle exercise with varied talk
Of what you've read, or heard, or liv'd or seen –
From this Fountain drink,
And, while drinking, think,
We should ne'er forget
The Donor's name – JOHN BRETT.

Ye ladies, who with fascinating smile,
Can make the desert bloom like paradise,
Ye who us men do of our cares beguile,
For whose regard we count not pains nor price –
From this Fountain drink,
And, while drinking, think,
We should ne'er forget
The Donor's name – JOHN BRETT.

The Poet's thanks, JOHN BRETT, your deed demands,
Ungrudgingly he sings your praise with rhyme;
May your good gift, unharmed by thoughtless hands,
Transmit your Saxon name to future times.
From this Fountain drink,
And, while drinking, think,
We should ne'er forget
The Donor's name – JOHN BRETT.

T. S. Gowing (1806-74)

The inscription at the base of the Fountain reads:

THE GIFT OF JOHN BRETT 1862

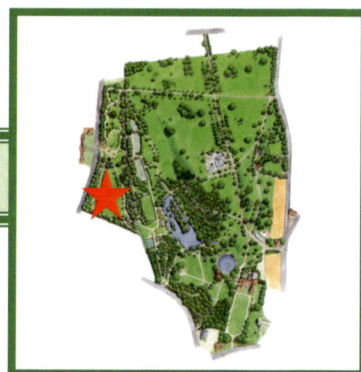

20. Arts and Crafts Shelter

Location: A short walk south from the Brett Drinking Fountain

Discussions for providing a shelter in the Public (Upper) Arboretum were first held at a Council meeting on 31 July 1867 when Cllr Henry Tunmer enquired as to whether "*any steps had been taken by the Arboretum Committee... to providing shelter from the rain in the public Arboretum*". In reply Cllr (and Arboretum Committee member) Henry Pearce stated that "*the subject had been brought before them, but they were of the opinion that it was undesirable to erect anything*". Tunmer countered that "*it seemed to him rather strange that the public Arboretum should be without any place of shelter from the sudden storms which sometimes came on, while in the private* [Lower] *Arboretum there was provision made*".

Despite this enquiry, the subject was not raised again until ten years later, at the Council meeting of 7 February 1877 when Cllr William Roe "*brought forward the old question of providing a shelter in the public Arboretum*"; again there were reservations. Alderman Edward Grimwade said that this matter had been before the General Purposes Committee again and again, and had been under consideration for a long time. He said that the question was: how many people should they provide shelter for? "*There were sometimes 400 or 500 people in the Arboretum at a time, and to provide a shelter for these would involve a very serious outlay. The committee had, therefore, come to the conclusion that they could not see their way to carrying out the improvement.*"

Roe raised the issue again three months later in May 1877. The Town Clerk replied that the matter "*had been before the* [General Purposes] *Committee several times, and several plans had been submitted to them, and opinions differed as to those plans, which in the opinion of some gentlemen involved too large an outlay*". The Clerk continued that the Surveyor had been asked to prepare a simpler scheme and he hoped that this would be reported on at the next meeting. However, it wasn't until the quarterly meeting of 8 May 1878, more than a year after Roe had resurrected the matter and 11 years after the original enquiry, that success looked imminent. The General Purposes Committee reported that "*In pursuance of the resolution of the Council, your Committee have considered the desirability of erecting a shelter in the Arboretum, and are of opinion that such a building will be a great convenience and comfort to persons frequenting the grounds. Your Committee recommended that a shelter be erected, and that it be referred to your Committee to obtain the construction of the building at a cost of not exceeding £150, that sum being the estimated cost thereof.*"

Still there was disagreement in the Council. The Mayor Charles Cowell said it was a question of whether the shelter was desirable or not. He thought it was best not to have one, but the majority of the committee were against him. Therefore the report was adopted and the controversial shelter was finally erected during August. It had taken more than a decade after it was first proposed and even then did not have the Mayor's approval.

So the Public (Upper) Arboretum had to wait much longer than the Private (Lower) to acquire a shelter but maybe it was worth the wait. The Victorian shelters in the Lower have long gone, but the Arts and Crafts Shelter (as it is now known) still stands today, 140 years later. The Friends of Christchurch Park hold their very popular annual Brass on the Grass concerts there every summer, even though (of course) it was designed and erected as a shelter, not a bandstand!

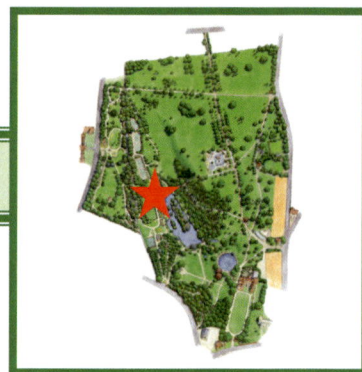

21. Armillary Sphere Sundial

Location: Butterfly Garden, Lower Arboretum

It is well-known that an armillary sphere sundial once adorned the Rock Gardens in the Lower Arboretum nearly one hundred years ago. It formed the centre-piece of the gardens on the North-west side of Wilderness Pond but was removed probably when the Rock Gardens were later redesigned and then displayed in the gardens at the back of Christchurch Mansion until it fell into disrepair. The sundial's plight was raised in August 2015 by Carrie Willis, a member of the Ipswich Museum Service who approached FoCP and in June 2016 after careful planning, FoCP launched an appeal to lead a project to restore and relocate it back to the Arboretum in memory of Dr John Blatchly MBE, MA, PhD, Hon LittD, FSA (1932-2015).

Scientist, musician, educator, historian and prolific writer, Dr Blatchly was a polymath and champion of Suffolk. Headmaster at Ipswich School from 1972-93, he was also instrumental in countless local projects including the erection of the Cardinal Wolsey statue on Curson Place, the restoration of "*the oldest ring of five bells in Christendom*" at St Lawrence church and reviving a number of the town's redundant medieval churches.

Fortunately, a good portion of the original sundial's stonework remained and could be saved. This was restored by Ray Templeton of Suffolk Masonry Services, who also provided new Portland stone where appropriate, using a number of David Miller's Arboretum postcards of the period to ensure that it matched the original feature. However, the original armillary was incomplete and badly damaged and so a new hand-made bronze Solstice armillary was sourced from Robert Foster of Telford. The project was funded by FoCP, Coes, Ipswich Borough Council, Ipswich School, The Friends of the Ipswich Museums, The Ipswich and Suffolk Club, The Ipswich Society, The Lord Belstead Charitable Settlement plus a number of individuals.

It was not practical to relocate the sundial to its original position in the Rock Gardens as this would have involved considerable landscaping work with existing sarsen stones and mature trees and shrubs. The new site chosen by David Miller is adjacent to the Rock Gardens and is a flat open area of grass next to the Butterfly Garden on the east side of the former croquet lawn. This is easily accessible next to the path for the public to enjoy and use.

The pedestal has been aligned to the cardinal directions and the setting-up of the pedestal and armillary was conducted under the supervision of Dr John Davis of the British Sundial Society. The unveiling of the restored sundial by His Worship The Mayor, Councillor Roger Fern was at midday on Thursday 5 January 2017. There is an on-site Information Board written by David Miller and designed by Martin Surgey of Lifechart and a free information booklet telling the story of the restoration and also written by David Miller is available at the RDVC.

Sundial statistics: The remains of the original sundial weighed 175 kg. Mr Templeton added 332 kg of new Portland stone together with a concrete foundation weighing 1,200kg, infill masonry of 100 kg and a pebble surround of 250 kg. The new bronze armillary weighs 10 kg and has a sphere diameter of 51 cm. In total this structure weighs over 2,000 kg (2 tons).

Did you know? Ipswich has a longitude of 1° 09′ 17″ East of Greenwich, which means that noon here is 4 minutes 37 seconds before noon at Greenwich!

The restoration, led by the Friends of Christchurch Park, of
The Armillary Sphere Sundial in Ipswich Arboretum
in memory of Dr John Blatchly MBE

Armillary Sphere Sundial c.1935

RESTORED AND RE-ERECTED
IN 2016 IN MEMORY OF
DR JOHN BLATCHLY MBE

49

22. Art in the Park

Location: Various locations, see map to the right

FoCP honoured the most famous resident of the Park, Mabel, by commissioning an oak chain saw sculpture and placing it in front of the oak tree on 29 September 2017, where she roosted and delighted visitors for so many years. The project was led by FoCP Secretary Sylvia Patsalides and the sculpture created by local tree surgeon David "Geordie" Good, owner of Green Man Tree Care. Good started experimenting with chain saw sculptures outside his workshop with left-over pieces of wood from tree felling work. These were spotted as potential exhibits for the Ipswich Arts Festival *Ip-art* and the rest is history. Good also has other pieces on display in the Park including two sculptures which can be found in the South-west corner near the lower Fonnereau Road entrance – *Clasped Hands of Friendship* (2008) and *Freedom!* (2009) (now sadly damaged). These were commissioned by the Parks Department and Ipswich Rangers and carved from ash trees on site which presented a risk of falling branches. Another piece, *Frog Bench* in the North-west area of the Park close to the top bridleway gate, was commissioned by a member of the public, whose late husband visited the Park daily. You will find plenty of Good's creations outside the Park too – an assortment of owls, hedgehogs, bears and griffins decorate private gardens in the area and further afield, seven mythical beasts can be found at Flatford (created for the RSPB) and a giant tortoise oak carving adorns the grounds of Rothschild House in Hertfordshire, where Lord Rothschild (1868-1937) famously rode one.

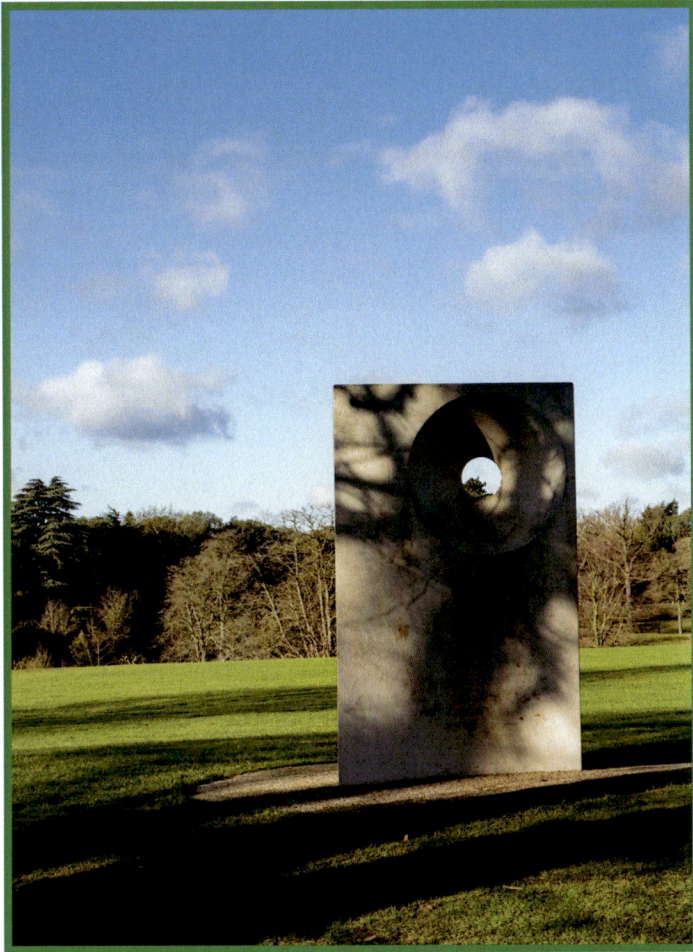

Innocence is a Portland stone monolith commissioned by Ipswich Borough Council as part of the HLF Restoration Project. It was carved in 2007 by Suffolk-based artist Linda Thomas, then newly graduated from Suffolk College. Located just to the North of the play area on the top of Snow Hill, the sculpture represents the artist's response to the restoration of the Park. Inspired by the windows in the main entrance to Christchurch Mansion, the artist decided to take a window into the Park. It contrasts people with the landscape, traditional with contemporary and new with old. Carved out of a single piece of Portland stone from Bowers Quarry in Portland, Dorset, an elegant tapered 'eye' to the top right reflects the pattern of light and shade from nearby trees and provides a running live video showing in one direction a traditional rolling landscape, and in the other, the fun and innocence of children at play. It is intended to be touched and is tactile, encouraging the viewer to interact with the piece.

The aluminium *Triple Mycomorph (Fungus Form)* sculpture by Bernard Reynolds can be found to the rear of Christchurch Mansion in the Wolsey Garden. It was commissioned in 1992 by World War II refugee and Ipswich resident Tom Gondris MBE as a memorial to his parents who perished in the Auschwitz-Birkenau concentration camp. The piece was originally made in plaster by Reynolds in 1953 but was later cast into metal in 1992 after Gondris visited Reynolds' studio to select a past piece of work which he felt symbolised "*the continuous resurgence of life*". Reynolds was born in Norwich in 1915 and trained at the Norwich School of Art. He exhibited with Henry Moore in 1936-37 and was formerly Lecturer in Charge of Three-dimensional Design at Suffolk College. A plaque below the sculpture reads:

THIS SCULPTURE IS DEDICATED BY TOM GONDRIS IN MEMORY OF HIS PARENTS EUGEN AND ELSE WHO DIED IN WORLD WAR II

51

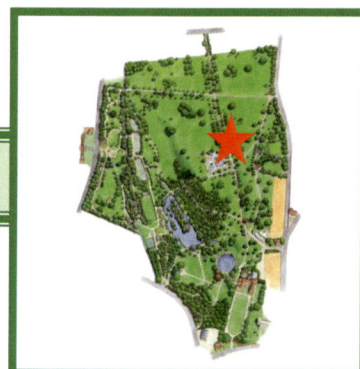

23. Burton Drinking Fountain

Location: North-east of the Children's Play Area

This drinking fountain is 34 years younger than the Brett Drinking Fountain and was donated by Sir Bunnell Henry Burton (1859-1943) in 1896 and restored in 2006. Like the Brett Fountain, the Burton Fountain has always stood at its present location, by the side of the Ancient Avenue close to the play area. Ipswich-born Burton was the eldest son of Henry May Burton, a wholesale grocer, and his wife Mary Bunnell née Lewis, and he became a director of the Ipswich firm Burton, Son and Sanders. He was organist of St Mary-le-Tower Church, Ipswich, Mayor of Ipswich (1905-06), and for 38 years (1905-43) was Chairman of the Governors at Ipswich School. In 1934 he was knighted for political and public services in Ipswich.

24. Cabman's Shelter

Location: Westerfield Road entrance

This shelter is Grade II listed and was built in 1892. It was originally located on the Cornhill and was created to provide a warm, dry space for Victorian drivers of horse-drawn cabs as they awaited their next fare in the centre of Ipswich. On 3 May 1895 it was towed by a steamroller from the Cornhill to the Park and placed north-east of the Round Pond near the Bolton Lane entrance to be used as a public shelter. One hundred years later in 1995 it was extensively damaged (80%) by fire following an arson attack by vandals. It was then covered by tarpaulin and left disused until it was removed to be restored as part of the HLF Restoration Project.

On 6 August 2006 after a year of hard work by craftsmen Peter Shemming and Robin Smy it was transported to its current location inside the Westerfield Road entrance to the Park from its restoration base at Hadleigh Road Industrial estate by a low-loader lorry. History was also remembered on 6 August as a steamroller and horse and cab accompanied the shelter on its journey via St Margaret's Green, Bolton Lane and Westerfield Road.

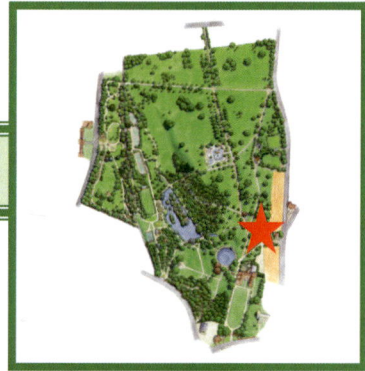

25. The Reg Driver Visitor Centre

Location: Bolton Lane entrance

Created as part of the £4.2 million HLF refurbishment of Christchurch Park, the Reg Driver Visitor Centre (RDVC) was opened on 6 May 2008 as a new, fully-staffed visitor and education centre, toilet facility (including a baby changing area) and offices on the site of the Park's previous Bolton Lane toilet block to the north of the Mansion. It was named after the first FoCP Chairman (1998-2003), also a former President and Chairman of the Ipswich Royal British Legion, and Ipswich Town Councillor, who died in 2007 aged 88.

As the centrepiece of the HLF Restoration Project the RDVC was designed to be as eco-friendly as possible and was packed with a number of green features including solar photovoltaic panels, two different depths of green roof, a biomass boiler, under-floor zoned heating, sun pipes and rainwater harvesting. The large windows on the south front were fitted with 'K' glass to allow heat and light into what is a heavily insulated building. The building won a High Commendation Award from the Ipswich Society in 2008.

The RDVC is open to the public seven days a week all year round, except Christmas Day and New Year's Day and is open from 10 am to 5 pm from May to August and from 10 am to 4 pm at all other times. The Park Manager is based in the centre and a receptionist is available throughout the day to answer any enquiries you may have. A large meeting room is available to hire for meetings and events and often has interesting displays of relevance to the Park. The reception can be contacted on 01473 433980.

26. Other Facilities and Events

Location: Various locations across the Park and Arboretum

Christchurch provides the winter venue for Ipswich parkrun, when the Chantry Park course becomes saturated. This is part of parkrun UK, free weekly 5km timed runs, with over 500 courses to choose from. Ipswich parkrun attracts visiting runners from all over the UK, and for those competitors who 'collect' different parkrun venues, Ipswich is one of only two parkrun locations in the UK starting with the letter 'I', the alternative being Inverness! Ipswich is therefore very well attended. FoCP recently received feedback from Ipswich parkrun that some visiting athletes ranked Christchurch in the top three parkrun locations in the UK. Other sports facilities here include five tennis courts, two outdoor table tennis tables, a full-sized bowling green and a pétanque piste. As well as the excellent and award winning RDVC, there is also a children's play area, a number of public toilets, and refreshments which are available at the hugely popular Pavilion Cafe (Kiosk), built in 1898, and located close to the play area (see photograph below), and Fonnereau's Tea Rooms at the rear of Christchurch Mansion.

The Park hosts many of the town's most popular events; those scheduled for 2018 were as follows: Ipswich to Felixstowe Historic Vehicle Road Run (6 May), Ipswich Fake Festival (9 June), Teddy Bear's Picnic (17 June), Ipswich Open Air Cinema (30 June), Ipswich Music Day (1 July), Pantaloons (4 July), Global Rhythm (7 July), Indian Summer Mela (8 July), FoCP's Brass on the Grass (in the Upper Arboretum on 15, 22, 29 July and 5 August), Ipswich Bubble Rush for St. Elizabeth Hospice (26 August), 11th Ipswich Scout Group Fireworks Display (3 November) and the Remembrance Day Service (11 November). FoCP also offers the following guided walks every year which during 2018 were: Spring Birdwalk (24 March), Dawn Chorus Walk (5 May) and two Bat Walks with the Suffolk Bat Group (1 and 15 September).

27. Spring

Follow us on: @Christchurch Park   @ChristchurchPk   www.focp.org.uk

28. Summer

59

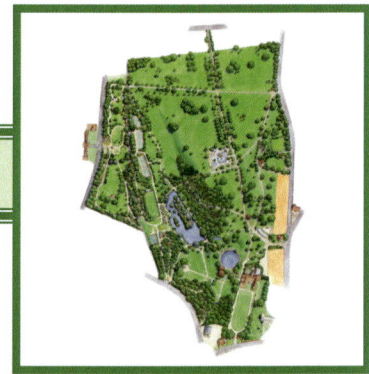

29. Autumn

30. Winter

31. Old Postcards

A selection from David Miller's personal collection of over 500 old postcards of Christchurch Park and Ipswich Arboretum.

Four views of the South Front of the Mansion. In the first image, there is so much ivy that the clock (added by the Fonnereaus in 1840) is partially obscured and the windows to the left are covered. G. R. Clarke wrote that when Lord Rochester visited he saw "*the park-keeper was driving two donkies attached to a large roller, for the purpose of keeping the turf smooth and level; and, that their hoofs might not penetrate the soil, he had contrived to put boots upon their feet*", inducing the Earl to observe that "*Ipswich was a town without people, that there was a river without water, and that asses wore boots.*"

65

Four views of the Round Pond formerly known as the 'Bason'. This pond is older than the Mansion and was probably one of the Priory fish ponds. The oldest of these images is the last one (with snow), ascertained by comparing the relative sizes of the Deodar Cedar (*Cedrus deodara*) which can be seen

in the centre of the last image, between the Pond and the Mansion, and which is still present today. To the right of the last image can be seen the back of the Queen Victoria Memorial which was unveiled on 28 May 1904 (see page 69 for a close-up view of the front of the statue).

Two pre-First World War postcards of the Wilderness Pond. Two Black-necked swans seen in the second image were a gift by Mayor Robert Stocker Paul in 1898 and came from a zoo in the Black Forest. Other birds here at this time included a Sarus crane, White stork, Peafowl and Egyptian geese.

68

The top image shows the Mansion's Great (also known as Banqueting) Hall, the main living room in Tudor times. Comparing it with page 7, one can see that little has changed. Below, the Queen Victoria Memorial was unveiled in 1904 but melted down during World War Two in 1942 to make munitions.

69

The top image shows the Park in c.1898 when sheep were a common sight. In G.R. Clarke's *History of Ipswich* (1830) he wrote that the Park was "*stocked with some peculiarly handsome deer, of a white colour, spotted with black.*" Below, a donkey at work with a snow plough in the Park.

70

The Wolsey Art Gallery was built in 1931 as a memorial to Cardinal Wolsey, who was born in Ipswich in or about 1475, and died at Leicester Abbey on 29 November 1530. Below, the Christchurch Park Memorial, now known as the Ipswich War Memorial was unveiled on 3 May 1924.

Two views of the Martyrs' Memorial; looking south and north. It was unveiled on 16 December 1903 by the Very Rev. Henry Wace, D.D., the Dean of Canterbury. In the first image can be seen Phipson's magnificent crocketted spire of St. Mary-le-Tower which rises to 53.5 metres (176 feet).

The above card was postmarked 1911 and shows the Pavilion Cafe (Kiosk), erected in 1898, dating this image between those two dates. Both of the oaks are still present. Below, the centre of this image shows the Cabman's Shelter which was towed by a steamroller from the Cornhill to the Park in 1895.

A march past by the Essex and Suffolk Cyclist Battalion on 13 May 1911 during the visit by The Right Hon. The Viscount Haldane, Secretary of State for War. Below, the Wolsey Pageant was staged in front of the Mansion from 23 to 28 June 1930 and visited by His Royal Highness the Prince of Wales.

Two structures no longer present in the Park. The above image shows the former shelter on the top of Snow Hill that was destroyed by fire in 1954. Note the wooden bell tower used to denote closing time. Below, the former bandstand was on the site of the current children's playground in the Park.

In these images of the Upper Arboretum there is no carpet bed, just a grass bank and potted plants which dates these photographs to before 1910. In the top image a man attends to the clock turret of the Arboretum Lodge, while below, note the magnificent Shakespearean Memorial Tree in the background.

In the top image a rustic bridge (no longer present) connects the Lower Arboretum to an island on the Wilderness Pond. Note the presence of *Gunnera*, which was reintroduced by David Miller in 2017. Below, the original Armillary Sphere Sundial. A footbridge can still be found in the foreground.

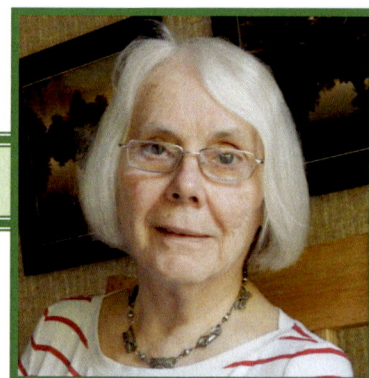

32. Scherenschnitte

Friends' member Erika Bülow-Osborne has over the last year delighted readers of FoCP's newsletter *The Christchurch Chronicle* with her regular contributions of exquisite artwork. Scherenschnitte means "scissor cuts" and is the art of cutting continuous paper designs. It is a tradition that can be traced back to Switzerland and Germany in the 1500s and Erika has been practising this art form since she was twelve years old. Her work demonstrates an historical link with the cut-paper creations of poet and artist Elizabeth Cobbold (nee Knipe, 1765-1824), second wife of Ipswich brewer John Cobbold (1746-1835), who famously created many scissor-cut paper Valentines at Holywells two centuries ago and which were also inscribed with poems of her own composition. Erika has amassed a wonderful collection of Scherenschnitte including trees, flowers, birds and insects, much of which she created following visits to the Park and Arboretum to photograph her subjects. The silhouettes are made from black paper which is gummed on the reverse and then placed onto white paper to highlight the typical outlines of the forms being studied. Erika was born in Germany and studied music and English at the University of Hamburg and Hochschule for Music. She taught at Luisen-Gymnasium Bergedorf, specialising in opera and musicals before moving to Ipswich. Her Scherenschnitte have been published alongside the work of poet and writer W. Kunze and in the cultural magazine *Lichtwark-Heft*. Erika is also part of the team at www.naturwelt.org/naturwelt-community/erika, where her scissor-cuts are published monthly. Erika's daughter Lois Cordelia is a prolific UK artist and illustrator in cut paper, acrylics and mixed media.

1. Arboretum Lodge, Ipswich School and Brett Drinking Fountain (see page 76)

2. Wolsey's Angels (see page 9)

Wolsey's Four Angels
Scherenschmitt Eila Bülow-Osborne
November 2017

3. Boer War Memorial (see page 18)

The Boer War Memorial
Scherenschmitt
Eila Bülow-Osborne
März 2017

4. Armillary Sphere Sundial (see page 49)

The Armillary Sphere Sundial
Scherenschmitt Eila Bülow-Osborne
März 2017

5. The Shakespearean Memorial Tree (see page 41)

The Blue Atlas Cedar . Old and New
Scherenschnitt
Erle Bülow Osborne
Juli 2017

6. Atlas Cedar (see page 33)

Cedar of Lebanon, Atlas Cedar Scherenschnitt Erika Bülow-Osborne Juli 2017

7. Giant Redwood (see page 33)

Wellingtonia Scherenschnitt Erika Bülow-Osborne Juli 2017

8. Deodar Cedar (see page 33)

Deodar Scherenschnitt Erika Bülow-Osborne Juli 2017

9. Mexican Weeping Pine

Pinus patula Patula Pine Pinus patula
Scherenschnitt Eila Bülow-Osborne
Mai 2018

10. Maidenhair Tree (see page 34)

Ginkgo biloba Maidenhair Tree Ginkgo
Scherenschnitt Eila Bülow-Osborne
Mai 2018

11. Purple Oakleaf Beech (see page 43)

Fagus sylvatica 'Rohanii'
Scherenschnitt Eila Bülow-Osborne
Mai 2018

12. Magnolia 'Galaxy'

Magnolia 'Galaxy'
Scherenschnitt Eila Bülow-Osborne
Mai 2018

13. Sweet Chestnut

Castanea sativa
Erika Bülow-Osborne

14. Horse Chestnut

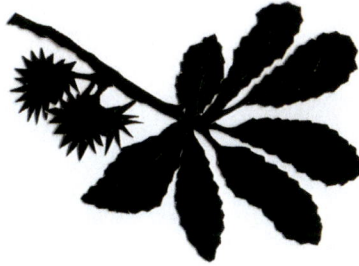

Aesculum hippocastanum
Erika Bülow-Osborne

15. English Oak

Quercus robus
Erika Bülow-Osborne

16. Common daisy

Gänseblümchen
Scherenschnitt
Erika Bülow-Osborne
März 2014

17. Cuckooflower

Wiesenschaumkraut
Scherenschnitt
Erika Bülow-Osborne
April 2014

18. Dandelion

Löwenzahn   Juni 2005
Scherenschnitt
          Erika Bülow-Osborne

19. Rosebay willowherb

Schmalblättriges
Weiden röschen
Scherenschnitt
Erika Bülow-Osborne
Januar 2014

20. Snake's-head fritillary

Schachbrettblume
Scherenschnitt
Erika Bülow-Osborne
März 2014

21. Stinging nettle

Brenn-Nessel
Scherenschnitt
Erika Bülow-Osborne
Januar 2014

22. Common Buzzard

Mäuse Bussard
Scherenschnitt   *Erika Bülow-Osborne*
Juli 2016

23. Common Swifts

Mauersegler
Scherenschnitt   *Erika Bülow-Osborne*
Juli 2013

24. Long-tailed Tits

Longtail Tits
Scherenschnitt
Erika Bülow-Osborne

25. Tawny Owls

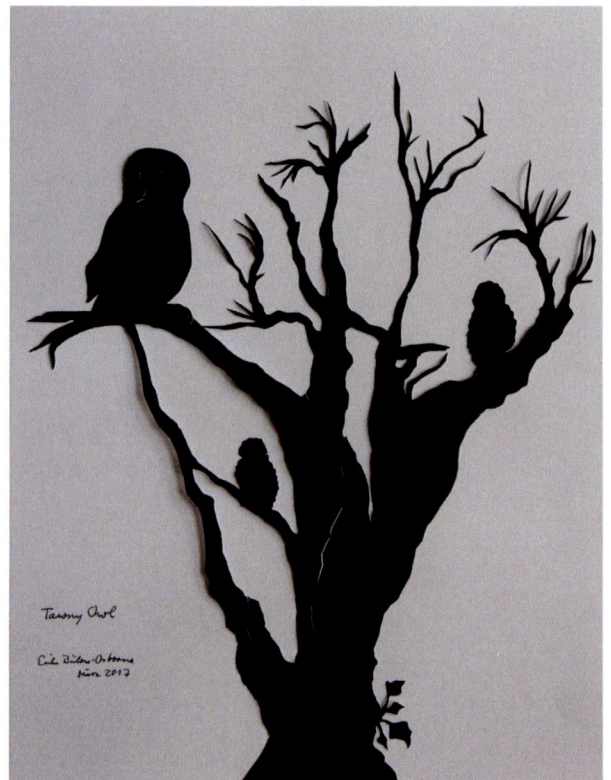

Tawny Owl
Erika Bülow-Osborne
März 2017

84

26. Swallow

Rauchschwalbe
Scherenschnitt
Juli 2013
Erika Bülow-Osborne

27. Blue Tits

Blue Tits
Scherenschnitt
Erika Bülow-Osborne

28. Goldfinches

European Goldfinch Distelfink
Scherenschnitt
Erika Bülow-Osborne
Osborn 2017

29. House Martins

Mehlschwalben
Scherenschnitt
Erika Bülow-Osborne
Juli 2013

30. Nightingale

Nightingale
Scherenschnitt
Erika Bülow-Osborne

31. Song Thrushes

Song Thrush
Scherenschnitt
Erika Bülow-Osborne

32. Sparrowhawk

Sperber
Scherenschnitt
Erika Bülow-Osborne
August 2016

33. Blackbird

Amsel
Scherenschnitt
Erika Bülow-Osborne
Oktober 2014

34. Nuthatch

Kleiber
Scherenschnitt
Erika Bülow-Osborne
August 2016

33. Christchurch Timeline

A selection of dates covering nearly one thousand years of history.

1086   *"In the said Borough, Alnulfus the priest has a church, Holy Trinity, to which belongs twenty-six acres in alms"* (Domesday Book).

c.1177   The Augustinian Priory of the Holy Trinity (also known as Christ Church) is founded a little anterior to 1177 and chiefly endowed by *Norman Gastrode fil Eadnothi*.

1297   Edward I visits Christ Church on the day of his youngest daughter Elizabeth's marriage to John I, Count of Holland.

c.1400   The Park's oldest tree, a yew located south-east of the Cenotaph, starts growing.

1536   Priory land and buildings are seized by the Crown with a value of £88 6s 9d, a victim of Henry VIII's dissolution of the monasteries. Most of the buildings are destroyed.

1545   Paul Withypoll, a prominent London Merchant, buys the Christchurch estate including St. Margaret's Church and some other land for £2,000.

1548-50   Christchurch Withypoll, later known as Withypoll House (now Christchurch Mansion) is built by Edmund Withypoll (Paul's son) on the site of the Priory ruins.

1561   Elizabeth I visits Christchurch (and again in 1579).

1567   The Wilderness Pond is created by Edmund Withypoll (also known as 'Dovehouse Pond'). The Park's springs previously fed other ponds and the town's water supply.

1645   Christchurch is inherited by the Devereaux family, Elizabeth and her husband Colonel Leicester Devereaux, who became 6th Viscount Hereford in 1649.

1668   Charles II stays overnight at the Mansion with Hereford and plays bowls in the Park.

1735   Claude Fonnereau, a successful London Merchant, buys the Christchurch Estate for £11,500. The Fonnereaus were descended from the Earls of Yvery in Normandy.

1735   John Kirby of Wickham Market, reports in *The Suffolk Traveller*, when referring to the last remains of the Priory's church, Trinity Chapel, that *"the strong foundation of this steeple was within these few years undermined and blown up with gunpowder"*.

c.1735   The Ice House is built.

1847   (9 November) Cllr James Allen Ransome first proposes both the idea and location of a plot of two fields known as 'Upper Bolton' to the west of the Rev. William Charles Fonnereau's Christchurch Park as a *"suitable place, in which a healthful and harmonious recreation could be carried out... beneficial to all classes of the town"*.

1851   Ipswich Arboretum is designed by Yorkshire nurseryman William Pontey and landscaping starts in March. It opens later that year to fee-paying subscribers.

1851   (4 July) Prince Albert visits the Fonnereaus at Christchurch Mansion after laying the foundation stone for the Grammar School (Ipswich School).

1851   (11 September) The first record of band playing in the Arboretum at the Ipswich Horticultural Society Fete by the Second Dragoon Guards, or Queen's Bays, a cavalry regiment then based in the town.

1853   The Rev. W. C. Fonnereau and *The Ipswich Arboretum Society* grants Ipswich Corporation a lease for the Upper Arboretum and it is opened to the public. The Corporation agrees a further lease with local nurseryman, William Brame Jeffries to "*maintain, preserve and keep up in good order*" the Public Arboretum and stock it with trees, shrubs and other plants. Jeffries was at full liberty to sell and remove stock from specified areas so long as they were replaced without delay. Fonnereau pays for two entrance lodges to be built, one at the Henley Road entrance opposite Ipswich School and the other (demolished in the 1950s) at the south-east bridleway entrance. These lodges were to be occupied by persons in the employment of Jeffries.

1859   David Storey is appointed first Arboretum Keeper. He resides in the Upper Arboretum Lodge and is paid 14 shillings per week to "*see that the Rules made by the Corporation for the preservation of the Arboretum and for the maintenance of proper conduct therein, are at all times observed.*" He stays in post until retirement in 1888.

1863   (10 March) The Prince's Oak is planted in the Arboretum.

1863   (1 May) The Brett Drinking Fountain is unveiled. Donated by John Brett (cost £64).

1864   (23 April) The Shakespearean Memorial Tree is planted in the Arboretum.

1869   The Suffolk Show takes place in the Park.

1878   (August) The Arts and Crafts Shelter is erected in the Arboretum.

1879   The Arboretum Lodge clock and turret is added (donated by George Green Sampson).

1892   William Neale Fonnereau puts the Christchurch estate on the market for £50,000.

1892   (19, 20 & 21 April) Ipswich Corporation consults the people of Ipswich with a local referendum of registered owners and ratepayers as to whether the town should purchase the Christchurch estate (by then reduced by Fonnereau to £42,000). 2,169 papers are returned blank, 87 spoiled, 5,110 votes against and 3,784 votes in favour.

1894   W. N. Fonnereau sells Christchurch for £36,000 to a property syndicate and part of the estate along Bolton Lane and Park Road is immediately resold and built upon.

1894   Felix Thornley Cobbold buys Christchurch Mansion and writes to the Mayor (23 October) "*Having contracted to purchase Christchurch House…, I desire to offer the property to the inhabitants of Ipswich as a free gift, subject to certain conditions.*" The conditions were that "*the main structure of the house be preserved in its integrity*", and that the Council purchase the remainder of the Park for the town. The offer is accepted and the gift completed on 23 February.

1895   (24 April) Christchurch Park is officially opened to the public.

1895   (3 May) The Cabman's Shelter is moved to the Park from the Cornhill.

1895   The stables and coach house at the Park Road entrance are designed by John Shewell Corder.

1896   (18 April) Christchurch Mansion opens as a local Archaeological Museum and Picture Gallery. In his will, from an estate of £407,790 15s 9d, F. T. Cobbold leaves a £20,000 trust fund to the Mayor and Burgesses of the Borough of Ipswich, the interest of which is to be used to preserve the building and purchase pictures and other works of art.

1896   The old Bolton Lane Lodge is demolished and a new one is built. The architect for the new lodge is J. S. Corder.

1896   The Burton Drinking Fountain is donated by Sir Bunnell Burton.

1898   The Soane Street Lodge is built. The architect is J. S. Corder.

1898   The Pavillion Cafe (Kiosk) is erected.

c.1900   Edward Henry Bostock's menagerie becomes a great public attraction in the Park.

1901   James Mann is appointed Head Gardener of the Upper Arboretum and resides in the Upper Arboretum Lodge. Mann would later become the Corporation's Parks

Superintendent but in the Arboretum he commences the annual carpet bedding display, a tradition which has continued to this day. He also inaugurates the Mayors' Walk and designs the Lower Arboretum Rock Gardens using sarsen stones that were discovered during the excavations for the Ipswich wet dock in the early 1840s.

1903	(16 December) The Martyrs' Memorial is unveiled.
1904	(28 May) The Queen Victoria Memorial is unveiled on the lawn in front of the Mansion. It is melted down during World War Two in 1942 to make munitions.
1919	(19 July) Peace Day celebrations include the planting of two oaks by the Mayor and Mayoress and an 'Aquatic Display' in the Round Pond by Ipswich Swimming Club.
1922	The Lower Arboretum is purchased by the Ipswich Corporation for £1,568 14s 3d.
1924	(3 May) Ipswich War Memorial (Cenotaph) is unveiled.
1924	The Boer War Memorial is moved to the Park from the Cornhill.
1924	A Tudor Merchant's house is moved from Major's Corner to the north of the Mansion.
1928	The Upper Arboretum is purchased by the Ipswich Corporation for £8,500.
1930	(26 June) The Prince of Wales visits Christchurch for the Wolsey Pageant.
1932	(19 October) The Wolsey Art Gallery is opened.
1940	(10 November) At 22.20 a kilo-Electron Incendiary Bomb lands in the Arboretum.
1941	(4 May) At 22.40 two 250 kg High Explosive Bombs land in the northern area of the Park approximately 200 yards apart (one at the bottom of Snow Hill) causing blast damage to at least 100 properties surrounding the Park including Ipswich School chapel's east window behind the altar which has its glass sucked out.
1983-86	Ipswich Arboretum plays a pivotal role in the town's successes in Britain in Bloom. As the centrepiece of the campaign the Arboretum helps Ipswich win the Regional Final on four consecutive years (1983-86), the English Final in 1986 and a prestigious award in 1985 for the best carpet-bedding display in Britain.
1986	The Peace Garden is opened (between the Wilderness Pond and the Cenotaph).
1987	(16 October) 235 trees are lost in the 'Great Storm': 40 in the Upper Arboretum (inc. six mature monkey puzzles), 8 in the Lower Arboretum and 187 in the main Park).
1988	The Bird Reserve (now known as the Wildlife Reserve) to the east of the Wilderness Pond is instigated as a result of the area being fenced off following the 'Great Storm'.
1988	An Armada Beacon is erected and lit in the Park (just north of the Ice House) to commemorate the 400th anniversary of the defeat of the Spanish Armada.
1995	The Cabman's Shelter is 80% destroyed by fire set by vandals.
1998	(25 March) The Cherry Walk is planted in the Upper Arboretum with twelve different ornamental flowering cherries, presented by the Ipswich Horticultural Society to commemorate 175 years of the Society.
2001	£150,000 refurbishment of the Play Area (Community Improvements Programme).
2003	The Heritage Lottery Fund approves an application for the Restoration of the Park.
2005-08	Implementation of the £4.2 million HLF Restoration Project (including the restoration of the Brett and Burton Drinking Fountains, Arts and Crafts Shelter, and Cabman's Shelter, the removal of silt in the Wilderness, Round, Horseshoe and Bog Ponds, the excavation and re-opening of the south tunnel-bridge connecting the Upper to the Lower Arboretum, top-dressing of paths, renovation of shrubberies, re-landscaping of flower beds, repairs to the drainage infrastructure, Park entrances, furniture and signs and the building of a new, staffed visitor and education centre).

2008 (6 May) The Reg Driver Visitor Centre is opened and the HLF Project completed.

2008-18 The Park is awarded the prestigious 'Green Flag' for eleven consecutive years.

2011 A £142,500 Lawn Tennis Association and Sport England grant enables the five tennis courts in the Lower Arboretum to be resurfaced.

2011 *Portrait of a Park* written by Reg Snook is published by Gresham and FoCP. Reg writes two further books *Portrait of an Owl* (2012) and *Portrait of the Birds* in collaboration with Philip Murphy (2014), both published by Gresham and FoCP.

2014 *Ipswich Arboretum – A History and Celebration* written by David Miller with photography by Liz Cutting is published by Gresham and FoCP.

2014-18 Rejuvenation of the tree collection. David Miller and Steve Leech plant over 200 new specimens in the Arboretum plus nearly one hundred more in the Park, worth over £60,000, nearly all of which are funded by individual sponsors, local businesses and organisations, including more than 130 new species and cultivars. Three new plantings guides are printed and botanical labels are provided (donated by FoCP).

2015 Constable's *Salisbury Cathedral from the Meadows*, 1831 at the Wolsey Art Gallery.

2015 (September) A new educational resource, the Outdoor Classroom, funded by the Papworth Trust (with a contribution by FoCP) is built by craftsman Richard King of the Magic Garden Shed Company using traditional early medieval methods. It is totally destroyed by fire set by vandals on 24 July 2017.

2016 A £1 million renovation of Christchurch Mansion includes the installation of additional CCTV cameras, repairs to the brickwork and roof, electrical rewiring and improvements to the heating and humidity to help preserve the artwork and artefacts.

2016 St Elizabeth Hospice '*Pigs Gone Wild*' event in the town during the summer sees *The Ham-inator* in the Upper Arboretum and *Captain Pigwash* and *Digby* at the RDVC.

2016 (22 July) The Queen's Oak is planted in the Park (donated by FoCP).

2016 *The Butterflies in Christchurch Park* written by Richard Stewart with photography by Liz Cutting is published by FoCP.

2016 (9 December) The new Arboretum Lodge clock is installed (donated by FoCP).

2017 (23 March) Air-spading to the Park's oldest tree, the English Yew located south-east of the Cenotaph. This is followed by further Air-spading and Terraventing to the Shakespearean Memorial Tree and the mature Giant Redwood (Wellingtonia) in the Upper Arboretum on 24 and 26 October (50% funded by FoCP).

2017 (30 August) Tree Information Boards by FoCP are erected next to the Park's oldest tree, the English Yew, and the Shakespearean Memorial Tree.

2017 (5 January) The restored Armillary Sphere Sundial is unveiled in memory of Dr John Blatchly MBE. The restoration is led by FoCP with a number of funding partners.

2017 (2 February) The Battle of Britain Oak is planted in the Park (donated by FoCP).

2017 (May) A Pétanque Piste is constructed in the Park (with a contribution by FoCP).

2017 (29 September) The oak Mabel sculpture is unveiled (donated by FoCP).

2017 (28 November) First record of Ring-necked parakeet (*Psittacula krameri*) in the Park.

2017/18 Benedetto da Rovezzano's *Wolsey Angels* at the Wolsey Art Gallery.

2018 In late 2018 a new fountain is scheduled to be added to the Round Pond. The project will be led by IBC with a number of funding partners, including FoCP.

2018/19 (24 November to 28 April) Auguste Rodin's *The Kiss* at the Wolsey Art Gallery.

34. The Friends of Christchurch Park

Location: Committee meetings are held at the RDVC

The Friends of Christchurch Park (FoCP) are a voluntary organisation formed in 1998 with 400 subscribing members. Our objectives are:

- to secure the preservation, protection and improvement of the Park as a place of historic and ecological interest, beauty, tranquillity, rest and recreation;
- to promote the conservation of the natural plant, animal and bird life in the Park;
- to encourage appropriate use of the Park through a range of activities;
- to educate the public in the history, natural history and other aspects of the Park.

We work closely with Park management and organise a number of free activities throughout the year to help achieve our aims. Our flagship events are our Brass on the Grass concerts held every summer on four consecutive Sunday afternoons in the Upper Arboretum. These concerts are free for everyone. We have published six books and also produce a newsletter *The Christchurch Chronicle* three times a year which is free to our members. We organise bird and bat walks in the Park and fund new and replacement trees in the Arboretum and Park including the Queen's Oak and The Battle of Britain Oak, both planted by His Worship The Mayor in 2016 and 2017 respectively. Recently we funded the new lodge clock in the Upper Arboretum in honour of George Green Sampson, the clock's original patron in 1879. We also led the recent restoration of the Armillary Sphere Sundial in memory of the late Dr John Blatchly MBE and re-erected it in the Lower Arboretum after an absence of nearly one hundred years.

Chairpersons of the FoCP:

- Reg Driver 1998 – 2003
- Robert Burlinson 2003 – 2007
- Shirley Sadler 2007 – 2008
- Richard Wilson 2008 – 2015
- Nichola Johnson 2015 – 2016
- David Miller 2016 – Present

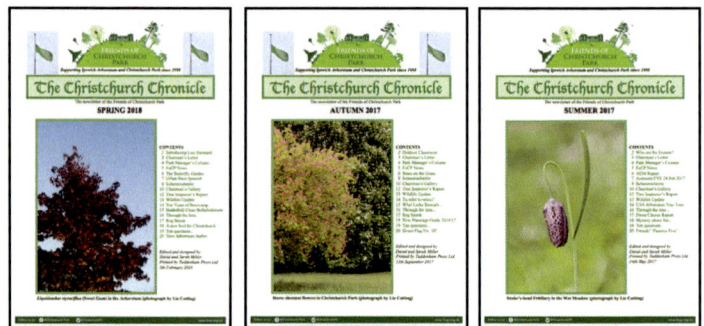

Anyone who shares our passion for the Park is welcome to join. Membership is by household, runs from 1 March to the end of February and costs £10 per year or £100 for lifetime membership. Corporate membership is £25. Please direct any new membership enquiries to the Membership Secretary and any other enquiries to the Secretary, FoCP, Reg Driver Visitor Centre, Christchurch Park, Ipswich, IP4 2EE.

35. Further Reading – FoCP Publications

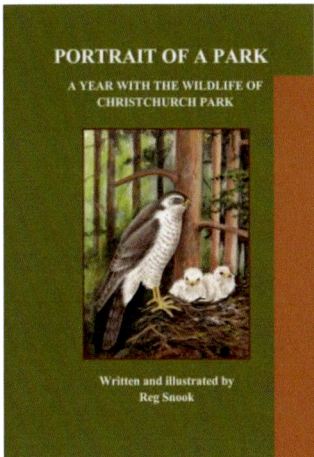

2011
£7.50
A5 80pp

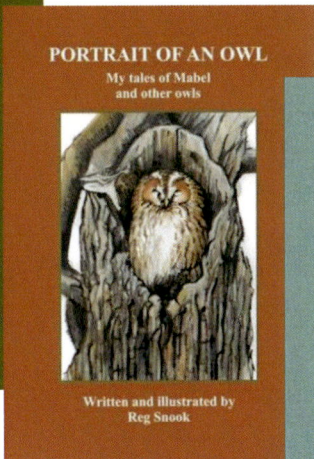

2012
£7.50
A5 80pp

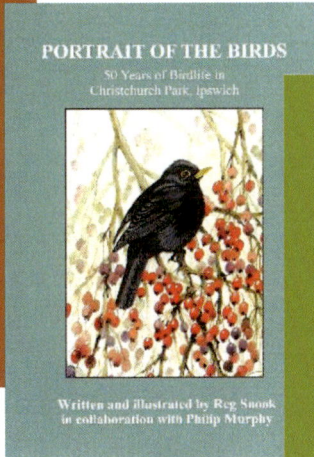

2014
£7.50
A5 80pp

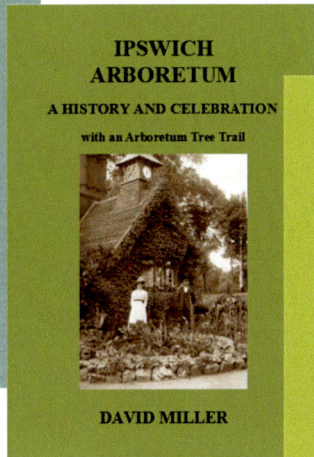

2014
£10
A4 162pp

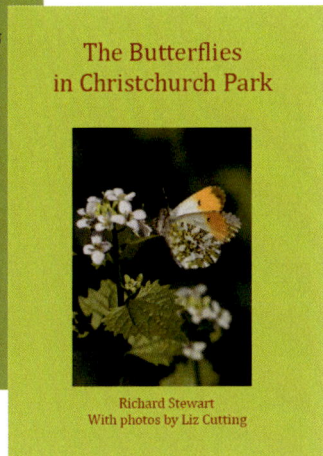

2016
£7.50
A5 80pp

All available at the RDVC
Proceeds benefit the Arboretum and Park

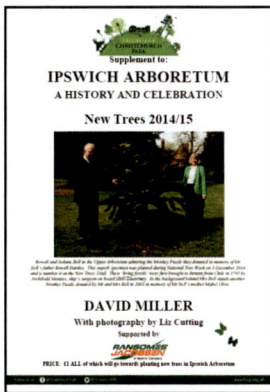

2015
£1
A4 8pp

2016
£1
A4 16pp

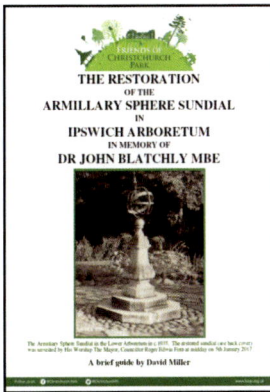

2016
FREE
A5 16pp

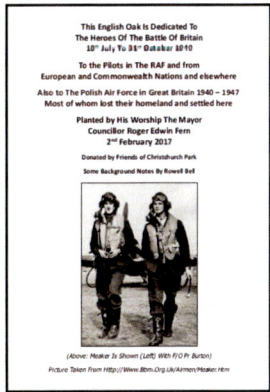

2017
FREE
A5 16pp

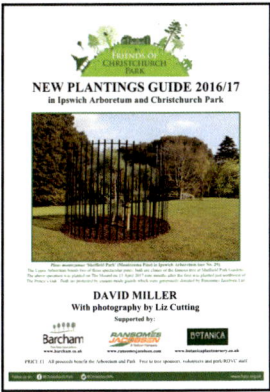

2017
£1
A4 24pp

2017
FREE
A4 and A3 poster available

ABOUT THE AUTHOR

David's connection with Christchurch Park goes back to his birth: he was born inside the grounds, in the Arboretum Lodge, and grew up in the Arboretum where his late father Tony was Head Gardener for a quarter of a century.

As Chairman of the Friends of Christchurch Park, David has overseen many projects to improve the town's favourite Park including the new lodge clock in the Upper Arboretum and the restoration of the Armillary Sphere Sundial in the Lower Arboretum. He has also planted over 300 specimen trees here, adding more than 130 new species and cultivars to the collection, and has labelled many of them.

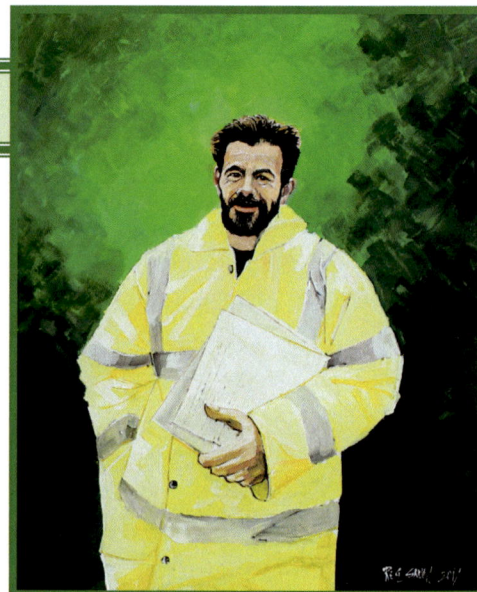

Portrait by Reg Snook, 2017

David is probably best-known however for one of his other passions: for over a decade he was Suffolk's leading long-distance runner, winning over 200 road, cross-country and track races across East Anglia and setting nearly 50 course records in the process.

A business studies graduate and business analyst by profession, David left behind the world of business information and now works in the horticulture industry. David's first book *Ipswich Arboretum: A History and Celebration*, published by Gresham and FoCP in 2014 is still available to purchase at the RDVC and Mansion and a number retail outlets in Ipswich.

ABOUT THE PHOTOGRAPHER

Liz took up photography in the mid-1990s and set up a darkroom in her cellar. She first worked exclusively in black and white, both 35mm and medium format, and her main subject matter was landscapes.

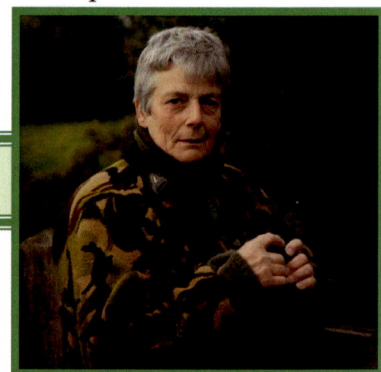

A keen naturalist, Liz decided to concentrate on nature photography a couple of years after buying her first digital camera in 2005. She rapidly became 'hooked', especially on birds, and cannot spend enough time out in the field. After taking early retirement from full-time employment in 2003 Liz worked part-time for the RSPB for over eight years, though she is now retired from all paid work. She still volunteers in the conservation sector and in particular is very involved with dormouse conservation in Suffolk and Essex.

Although sometimes travelling around the UK and abroad, much of Liz's photography is local, particularly around Suffolk and north Essex. Like many nature photographers, she prefers to be out on her own and tries to find quiet places and avoid busy times. A regular on the national and international photography exhibition circuit, Liz's images have been used by the RSPB, Suffolk Ornithology Group, Suffolk Naturalists' Society, Colchester Natural History Society, the Hawk and Owl Trust and the British Trust for Ornithology, and have appeared in local and national newspapers, in journals, on Christmas cards and in the Bird Atlas 2007-11.

INDEX

Numbers in **bold** indicate an illustration.

L

M

N

O

P

PERFECT EVERY BLADE.

The Ransomes TR320.

A WALK IN THE PARK.

The TR320 is one of the lightest machines on the market, meaning parks and ornamental areas are kept pristine. The ability to cut and collect ensures a clean finish and keeps clippings away from paths.

The winning combination of narrow transport width, a productive width-of-cut, plus superior slope capabilities and manoeuvrability, allows you to safely navigate the tightest of spaces and most challenging terrain.

To find more information and to book a demonstration, please contact your local dealer.
www.ransomes.com

RANSOMES®

ONE MOWER.
EVERY SITE.
JOB DONE.

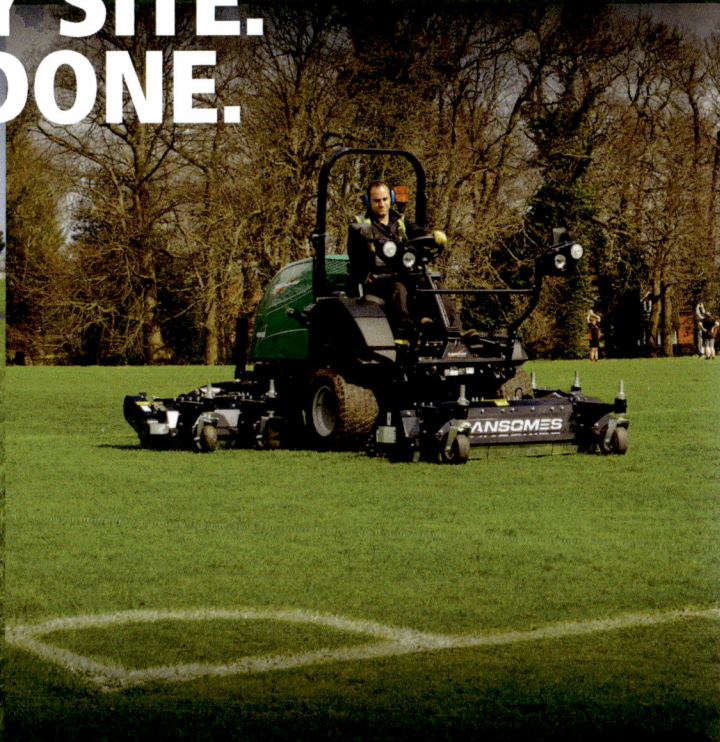

The Ransomes HM600.

The HM600 has been built in collaboration with Müthing to deliver a robust, reliable mower with the ability to tackle the toughest jobs, and the finesse to manoeuvre tight spaces while providing a quality after-cut appearance. From a clean, fine, rolled finish across sports pitches to routine cuts, the HM600 leaves an even spread of mulched clippings. It also tackles the irregular cuts, bringing the lesser maintained areas back under control.

HM600

**Visit www.ransomesHM600.com
to watch the machine working and
book a demo with your local dealer.**

Surgey, Martin, 41, 48
Sweet Chestnut, 12, **13**

T

Table tennis tables, 55
Teddy Bear's Picnic, 55
Templeton, Paul, 17, 48
Tennis Courts, 55, 89
Terence, 11, 30, **31**
Terraventing, 41
Thingstede Way, 5
Thomas Wolsey: Ipswich's Greatest Son (exhibition), 8
Thomas, Linda, 51
Toft, Albert, 18
Treaty of Versailles, 17
Tree Information Boards, 41, 89
Triple Mycomorph, **51**
Tudor merchant's house, 88
Tulip Tree, **34**
Tunmer, Henry, 46
Turkish Hazel, **43**
Turner's Oak, **43**

U

Upper Bolton, 32, 86
Upper Brook Street, 11

V

Viscount Haldane, The Right Hon. The, 74

W

Wace, Very Rev. Henry, 15, 72
Ward, Thomas, 37
Webb, Rear Admiral Sir Richard, 16
Western Red Cedar, **34**
White stork, 19, 68
Wilderness Pond, 10, **11**, 14, 30, 48, **68**, 86, 88, **back cover**
Wildlife Reserve, 88
William the Conqueror, 5
Willis, Carrie, 48
Wilson, Richard, 90
Wingfield, Sir Humphrey, 5
Winter, **62**, **63**
Withypoll, Edmund, 4, 5, 6, 11, 86
Withypoll, Paul, 5, 86
Withypoll, Sir William, 6
Wollemi Pine, **34**, 42
Wolsey Angels, 8, 89
Wolsey Art Gallery, 8, **9**, **71**, 88, 89
Wolsey Garden, 51
Wolsey Pageant, 8, **74**, 88
Wolsey, Thomas, 8, 71
Wren, **21**
Wright, Bill, 44
Wryneck, 19